BE STILL

AND

take a bubble bath

52 Calming Devotions for Women

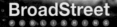

BroadStreet
PUBLISHING

BroadStreet Publishing Group, LLC.
Savage, Minnesota, USA
Broadstreetpublishing.com

Be Still and Take a Bubble Bath

© 2020 by BroadStreet Publishing®

978-1-4245-6077-6
978-1-4245-6078-3 (eBook)

Entries composed by Michelle Cox and Julie Lavender.

Design by Chris Garborg | garborgdesign.com
Editorial services by Michelle Winger | literallyprecise.com

Printed in China.

20 21 22 23 24 25 26   7 6 5 4 3 2 1

Introduction

Most of us are under so much stress we are like a rubber band that's been stretched to the limit. Like that rubber band, we're going to either snap back or break if we add more stress. We know we're too stressed, but what are we supposed to do about it?

Sometimes those anxieties are from our own doing as we over-commit, taking on enough responsibilities and challenges to exhaust a dozen women. Other times they are from things that are completely out of our control—which adds a whole other layer of stress because we like to be in control, don't we?

That's what *Be Still and Take a Bubble Bath* is all about. There are 52 devotions to help calm and relax us during our stressful days. It's truly amazing how many stressors there are in our lives, and they can wreak havoc emotionally and even cause serious health problems if we let them go unaddressed.

We'll talk about learning to say no when asked to take on tasks. (Yes, it can be done. Really.) We'll discuss letting God be the keeper of our calendars. And we'll talk about stressful situations we might encounter—and what to do about them.

Take a long, luxurious bubble bath. Soak your cares away as you take your eyes off your problems and put them on Jesus. He doesn't want any of us to be stretched beyond our limits.

I Can Do That

Every good and perfect gift is from above,
coming down from the Father of the heavenly lights,
who does not change like shifting shadows.

JAMES 1:17 NIV

Lauren's Facebook posts make all her girlfriends a bit jealous. Lauren is a busy author. She jets around the world doing research for her historical novels. She's a guest on television shows, does radio interviews, and meets fascinating people. Her fun personality draws people to her, and she's usually surrounded by adoring fans. She's thin, gorgeous, and has beautiful fashionable clothes. But all these things aren't what makes her friends jealous.

It's her bubble baths that set off the green-eyed envy.

Every once in a while, Lauren posts photos of her jetted tub filled to overflowing with bubbles. Lit candles all around the tub's ledge cast a warm and welcoming glow. And Lauren usually always mentions what soothing music she's playing for her leisurely bubble-bath soak.

Most of us do well to get a quick shower or zoom through the tub as if we're being timed for world-record speed. We have too much to do. Taking time to relax? That's a joke. Or is it?

You see, Lauren's one of the busiest people around. Her to-do list probably stretches from South Carolina all the way to California. But she's discovered something important that we'd all be wise to learn. Lauren paid attention when she read in God's Word that he designed our bodies to need rest.

Her bubble baths aren't wasted time. They allow her body to rest, to relax, and to rejuvenate so that she will be refreshed for the important tasks God has given her to do. She's taking care of the temple God gave her so that she'll be ready whenever God opens doors for her.

Let's try something new this week. Let's take twenty minutes for ourselves and enjoy a bubble bath. Let's rest the bodies God gave us and spend some time relaxing. Break out the candles. Put on some soft music. Let the bubbles and warm water soak your cares away. You can do it. Just think of this refreshing time as a good gift from the Father who loves you.

Father, I take great care of everyone else, but I'm sure not too good when it comes to taking care of myself. If I'm honest, I'm terrible about doing that. Remind me to slow down and to make time to care for the body that you've given me. I want to fulfill all the plans that you have for me, but I can only do that if I'm in good shape physically, emotionally, and spiritually. Help me to quit pushing myself to ridiculous extremes and to realize that an occasional bubble bath soak isn't a guilty luxury, but a way to care for myself so I'll be refreshed and able to do more for you.

Why don't you take time to enjoy a bubble bath? How can you become a better caretaker of the physical body that God has given to you?

Taking baths improves your mood, decreases your stress, promotes better sleep, and relieves muscle pain. One study found that a daily bath, usually at the end of the day, significantly improved the mood and optimism of the participants.

Proof of Goodness

*You keep him in perfect peace whose mind is stayed on you,
because he trusts in you.*

Isaiah 26:3 esv

Tina carefully opened the box. Her grandmother had passed away several weeks back, and these were the things she'd wanted Tina to have. Tina's grandmother had been her best friend, so she was excited—and a bit emotional—to see what was inside.

When she opened the box, she realized it held the greatest treasure her grandmother could've left her—her grandmother's Bible. Held together with duct tape and with pages falling out from use, the Bible still had a faint scent of her grandmother's favorite perfume. Tina could see that countless verses were underlined with notes written beside them of times God had been faithful or answered her prayers.

Her grandmother's prayer journals were also there. Written almost like a diary, they described the stress-filled moments when the children were small, scary moments when the kids were sick with high fevers, anxieties when finances ran short and when the weather ruined the crops, and other struggles.

But the journals also held notes about answered prayers—like a bumper crop of corn one summer that was enough to share with two neighbors, a beautiful wedding for Tina's mother, provision of safety during the tornado that touched down close to the farm, and the fellowship of family and friends at Christmas. Yes, tense moments dotted the journal, but grateful moments flooded the pages, too.

Did you know that keeping a gratitude journal can be a beneficial stress-reliever? Writing a list at the end of each day of all the things God did for us can serve as a reminder that he cares for us and will handle the things in life that cause us stress. When we journal answers to prayers or unmerited blessings and favor, we're reminded how much God loves us and how he always takes care of us. Those journals will be a priceless gift to leave behind for our children and grandchildren—reminders that God hears us when we pray, and that he always answers.

Keep a journal beside the tub. After slipping into a warm bubble bath, scribe words of God's goodness and give him praise.

God, thank you for the legacy of my parents, grandparents, and others who taught me what it means to follow you and to recognize that every good gift comes from you. Help me live a grateful life as well, one that will be a legacy for those who come after me. Remind me that I'm less anxious when I am dwelling on you and your goodness instead of my problems. Please help me as I go about my day to keep my mind on you, watching for ways that you work in my life and the lives of others around me. Help me to learn to write those things down, or at least make a mental note of them, so I can have a heart of gratitude.

How will keeping a journal of God's
faithfulness and goodness give you peace?
What's your favorite thing you've written
in your journal? Can you share that with
someone who needs to hear about
God's goodness?

People who make a concerted effort to practice an attitude of gratitude each day reap many benefits, like the fact that stress hormones like cortisol are twenty-three percent lower in grateful people. Additionally, those who keep notes in a journal or some other form of daily gratitude practice can actually reduce the effects of aging to the brain.

CHAPTER THREE

Bubbles and Giggles

*He will once again fill your mouth with laughter
and your lips with shouts of joy.*

JOB 8:21 NLT

Giggles echoed from the master bathroom. The two little girls, Kate and Melissa, were having bath time in the oversized tub. They loved their cousin time, and bubble baths were always a must-do at the end of the evening when they had a sleepover.

Bubbles floated up to their necks. Each had designed bubble hairdos and bubble beards on the other, and their handiwork sent them into squeals of laughter. They dove into the water, disappearing into the mounds of bubbles.

Once they tired of that, they had a bubble blowing contest, catching large bubbles on their hands and then blowing them into the air. They watched in fascination as the bubbles floated across the bathroom before they burst.

They took heaping handfuls of bubbles and made fancy designs on the side of the tub. Then they turned to Kate's mom, Betsy, who sat across the bathroom watching them to make sure they were safe. Kate said, "Mama, make us a new hairdo. I want a bun and Melissa wants a ponytail."

She knelt beside the tub, scooping handfuls of bubbles in her hands, and soon the two cuties sported a bubble messy bun and a long bubble ponytail. Their laughter pealed out, especially when they realized that Betsy was now as wet as they were, her jeans and shirt soaked by two little girls splashing around in the bubbles as if they were playful dolphins.

It was so worth it as Betsy soaked in the sweetness of her daughter and niece and whispered a prayer of thankfulness to the God who'd loaned them to her. They both were pure joy. And even though Betsy wasn't actually in the bubble bath, sharing their merriment had removed all the stress of the day.

Maybe you need to take a few moments tonight to thank God for his blessings to you. For a home and a tub for silly girls and bubble baths. For sweet laughter that rings throughout the room and into your heart. And for the stress-busting power of contagious joy.

Father, thank you for the gift of family. For bubble baths and sweet laughter that soaks into my heart and makes me smile. Even though family can be the source of my stress and exhaustion throughout the day, it only takes a few moments of laughter to make it all worth it and for my stress and tiredness to disappear. Lord, I want to have that same kind of happy spirit as I serve you. Please give me the kind of joy that is contagious.

Has laughter been missing from your life? What can you do to bring the joy of Jesus into your day? How can you be contagious so others will want to meet him?

A good laugh has great short-term effects. When you start to laugh, it doesn't just lighten your load mentally, it actually induces physical changes in your body.

CHAPTER FOUR

Resting

May the God of peace, who through the blood of the eternal covenant brought back from the dead our Lord Jesus, that great Shepherd of the sheep, equip you with everything good for doing his will, and may he work in us what is pleasing to him, through Jesus Christ, to whom be glory for ever and ever. Amen.

HEBREWS 13:20-21 NIV

Goldilocks had the right idea—neither extreme worked for her. She chose the one that was just right. A bubble bath at the end of a long and stressful day should be the same way, not too hot, not too cold, but just right.

The same is true of social and civic commitments. Too many commitments cause us anxiety and stress and result in poor performance in one or more areas of our lives. Often that's the area that affects our family. We might wish we could be a superwoman and do it all, but we can't.

Something will suffer—our health or our family's well-being, a relationship with a friend, or maybe even our position at work. Saying yes too frequently can lead to anger and resentment if that yes causes us unnecessary stress or makes us put our family in second place.

Before giving an automatic yes to a request, we need to learn to first say, "Let me pray about that decision." Sometimes saying yes is the easy way to keep peace or get the job done. But at times, saying yes means robbing someone else of the blessing of taking on that role or responsibility.

We need to pray diligently, read God's Word, and seek counsel from mentors if necessary before making a decision that might over-commit us. And to abide in his will, we just might have to learn to say no more often.

On the flip side, too few commitments don't benefit us either. God commands us to serve others. Even if we're busy with work and family, we need to seek a balance so that we can still find ways to bless and help those around us in some manner. Volunteering at places like homeless shelters, fostering organizations, classrooms, or church takes our mind off the stresses in our lives and brings a peace that comes from obedience to God's instructions. Helping others helps us even more.

Find a balance. As you settle into the bubble bath, know that your commitment status, like the temp of the bath water, is just right.

Dear God, sometimes I over-commit myself, causing great angst and stress. Help me learn to say no when the task is not your will for me. And then, God, I have seasons when I'm not committed enough to the things that you want me to do. Help me to say yes to those things and to serve with a glad heart. Father, there are sometimes moments when I don't really feel like I have a choice when it comes to saying yes to still another obligation. In those times, comfort and guide me. For the times I can control, Lord, help me to know that my commitments are balanced just right.

Why do you think it's hard for you to say no? Do you feel over-committed or under-committed in this season of your life? What can you do to change either situation?

Feeling overwhelmed because of an overcommitted schedule tends to lead to feelings of despair, powerlessness, and anxiety. Without a healthy and quick resolution, that kind of stress can affect a person emotionally and physically and cause a decline in health.

CHAPTER FIVE

Beauty Treatments

Before a young woman's turn came to go in to King Xerxes,
she had to complete twelve months of beauty treatments
prescribed for the women, six months with oil of myrrh
and six with perfumes and cosmetics.

ESTHER 2:12 NIV

Can you imagine being part of the world's biggest beauty pageant? As a Jewish orphan, I imagine it was quite intimidating for Esther to suddenly be placed in this position to possibly be the next queen. Talk about stress.

But Esther also had some pretty awesome things going on. She had twelve months for beauty treatments. That's pretty mind-boggling to most of us who rush through five to ten minutes each day to slap on some make-up.

Esther had special foods chosen just for her. Foods which would make her look healthy and cause her skin to glow. She had seven attendants to help her. Imagine how good we could look with a year of beauty treatments and seven women to help us with hairstyles, fashion advice, and with choosing what cosmetics to use.

I'm sure that part was fun for Esther, but surely she must have been anxious about whether or not the king would think she was beautiful or if she'd please him.

The Bible says that the women had six months with oil of myrrh and then another six months with perfumes and cosmetics. The best of everything was available for them. Surely some scented baths were included in Esther's beauty routine. To relax her. To treat her skin so it was smooth and blemish-free. And to ease any stress and anxiety she was going through.

Esther was outwardly beautiful, but more importantly, she was beautiful on the inside where it truly counted. That's what set her apart from the other women. Esther had a willing spirit to do whatever God wanted her to do.

Some of us might not be outwardly beautiful, but we can all work to attain a beautiful and willing spirit for God. He might ask us to do some big tasks which—like in Esther's situation—cause anxiety or stress. But as we seek to live for him, that's another great way to use our bubble bath time— to pray about our concerns and situations and give them to God. There's not a better stress reliever than Jesus.

Lord, I love what you say about Esther, that she was brought to the palace for such a time as this. Even though she had to be afraid and stressed about what you had called her to do, she trusted you and had a willing heart. Give me the courage and obedient heart of Esther. I want to accomplish the big tasks you have for me, the for-such-a-time-as-this moments. I'll admit I have anxiety because I don't seem capable of fulfilling your plan for me. Just as the water from my bubble bath goes down the drain, wash those fears and anxieties away from me and make me full of courage for you.

Bubbles eventually dissolve and swirl down
the drain. How can God wash away the
fear and stress from you?

Relaxing in a nice hot bubble bath sounds like the perfect way to commemorate National Bubble Bath Day, which is celebrated annually on January 8th.

CHAPTER SIX

Catching Up

As iron sharpens iron,
so a friend sharpens a friend.
PROVERBS 27:17 NLT

Can you remember how much fun you had on the playground with an elementary school friend? Think back to middle school sleepovers—weren't they just the bees' knees? And what about late night gab sessions with the bestie in high school? Didn't everything feel better when you told your problems to your favorite confidante?

Good friends are good for the heart. And our health. And not only when you were just a kid, teenager, or college student. Adults need interactions with other adults—they need friends.

A best friend or a small, core group of great friends reduces stress and boosts happiness by giving us a sense of belonging and purpose. Friends help us to cope with difficult times, such as a serious health situation, the illness or death of a parent or loved one, a divorce, or the loss of a job. In turn, we can help our friends through difficult times too. Close friendships give us the opportunity for prayer partners and spiritual mentors.

As busy people, we often drift away from personal friendships, citing a lack of time. Yet, it's important that we make time. We can grab a quick lunch, meet for coffee, take a walk over a lunch break, or run errands together on a Saturday morning.

Though face-to-face personal contact is best, when we absolutely can't find the time to leave the house, we can catch up with friends as part of our bubble bath routine. We can chat on the telephone while soaking or connect with a lengthy text exchange. If our commitments don't allow enough time for a bubble bath on a particular night, a shorter—but oh-so-relaxing—foot bath can wash away stress and give us a few spare moments to reach out to that friend.

It's hard to feel stressed when we've spent a couple of hours catching up with our besties, lifting one another up in prayer, and sharing about the goodness of our amazing God.

Dear God, you have blessed us with the gift of friendship in a circle of love. Help me to be intentional to stay connected with those friends that you've placed in my life. I thank you that my friends love me despite my flaws—a tiny glimpse of your perfect love for me. Help me to also be supportive and encouraging to my friends to bear witness of your love. I realize you haven't given me my life experience for it to go to waste, so help me to be a mentor to the younger women, and to share what you've taught me through the years. Let our friendships serve to sharpen one another, pressing us on to a closer relationship with you.

Do you know what's at the top of your friends' prayer requests right now? Have you asked each friend if there's something you can do to help (besides praying for them)?

Soaking your feet in warm water for twenty minutes a day calms the mind and relaxes the body. Foot baths increase the overall body temperature, relaxing muscles and tension, and alleviating stress. Mood-boosting footbaths lower blood pressure and improve sleep habits.

Overflow

Let everyone who is godly offer prayer to you at a time when you may be found; surely in the rush of great waters, they shall not reach him. You are a hiding place for me; you preserve me from trouble; you surround me with shouts of deliverance.

PSALM 32:6-7 ESV

The Andersons loved helping with their church's college-aged singles. They had a great group, but one young man (we'll call him Dale) wasn't as mature as the others—which led to some interesting moments.

Sandy and Bob rented two big cabins and took the singles to the mountains. The weekend was a time of precious fellowship with worship sessions each morning and evening. They did fun things each day, but they all loved the evenings at the cabins where they could play pool, enjoy the fireplace, and just be together.

There were huge tubs in the bathrooms of the cabin—and that's where one of those never-to-be-forgotten moments with not-as-mature-as-the-others Dale took place. While everyone else hung out together, Dale decided to enjoy the jetted tub in his room on the third floor of the cabin.

There are two things you need to understand. Dale was a large guy. And when he did something, he was totally absorbed in it. Dale turned the faucet to fill the tub. Soon the water was bubbling. He filled it full before he got in. When he did, his extra girth made water overflow, but Dale didn't notice. From what they heard later, his inner dolphin took over and he dove repeatedly into the foaming water. As the water in the tub dwindled, he added more.

Soon the guys in the second-floor bedroom noticed that water was dripping on them. At first, just drops, and then a steady trail of water. Dale's tub had overflowed into their lives, and they had to jump into action quickly to fix the situation.

All of us have likely had life overflow on us. Sometimes it can feel as if we've been deluged with out-of-control situations, and the stress just keeps on coming. We're so blessed, because, just as the guys took action quickly to stop the overflow, we have a God who can take charge of those difficult times that overwhelm us.

Are you stuck in an overflow of circumstances today? Take it to the one who will have no trouble stopping it.

Lord, sometimes I feel as if my life is filled to overflowing with problems that I can't fix. I'm stressed and overwhelmed by that, and I often feel that I can't even get my head above water and am going down for the third count. I've learned that when I'm drowning in hard times, you are the one who can lift me from my circumstances, who can stop the flow of troubles. I'm so grateful that whenever I'm overwhelmed, I can come to you. I've learned that even if the flood of problems doesn't go away, just knowing that you're there with me makes all the difference in how I view each day.

How does it affect you when you feel like you're drowning in difficult situations? What difference does it make to know that God is there with you in those circumstances?

While difficult times can feel like a deep dark hole that we can't escape and we often wonder "Why is this happening to me?" there is a silver lining to tough times. It's through the difficult times in our life, that we are able to grow.

CHAPTER EIGHT

Breath of Life

The Spirit of God has made me,
and the breath of the Almighty gives me life.

JOB 33:4 ESV

When a dive master works with new scuba diving students, he stresses the importance of breathing. Breathing? Wait, we all breathe. It's a natural thing. What is there to learn about breathing? A lot, apparently, if you're taking a plunge into deep waters. Dive masters focus on the difference between a big breath and a deep breath. A big breath means sucking in lots of air, affecting buoyancy, but a deep breath directs oxygenated air into the bottom of the lungs, replacing as much used air as possible.

Deep breathing is beneficial to more than just scuba divers. Studies show that taking deep breaths is effective for a person's well-being. When we think back to science lessons as a kid, we know that breathing delivers oxygen to every cell in the body. That includes all the vital organs as well as the brain. Deep breathing raises blood oxygen levels—increasing calmness, improving mental alertness, and alleviating stress.

Fast shallow breaths lead to stress, anxiety, and tiredness. Scuba students practice breathing slowly and deeply. Dive masters encourage them to take a deep breath and appreciate the beauty of the underwater world before taking another breath. Sounds like something that would benefit those of us above the water too, right?

When God breathed the first breath of life into Adam, the Bible says Adam became a living being. We have the very breath of God in our bodies. God wants us to take a deep breath into the lungs he created and slowly exhale, taking in the beauty of the world around us.

He doesn't want us to take fast, shallow, stressed-out breaths. He wants us to breathe in his goodness. To fill our lungs, hearts, souls, and bodies with him. With our lungs and bodies filled to capacity with the breath of God, our cares and worries seem to dissipate. We can lavish in the glory of God and know that we're in his hands.

Scuba divers or not, let's take deep breaths every day, inhaling slowly and exhaling slowly, giving every one of our cares to God.

Heavenly Father, thank you for the breath of life. The air inside my lungs at this very moment belongs to you. You gave me life, Lord, and I am grateful. You want me to be filled with you. To know you and to make you known. Help me breathe you in deeply, knowing that my life depends on you. And with every breath I exhale, let it be for your glory. Help me to breathe life into those around me with your breath, your words, and your goodness. Let your breath calm and soothe me, Lord, so that I might serve you better. When life gets tough, help me take a deep breath and put my trust in you.

Think about God breathing life into your lungs. How can that image promote calmness after a stressful day? Now think about sitting close enough to Jesus to hear him breathing. How can that bring you peace during a difficult time?

Tourists come from all over the world to bathe in the Dead Sea, bordered by Israel on one side and Jordan on the other. Known for its therapeutic properties, the Dead Sea is so high in salt and mineral content that bathers can't actually swim— they float on top with little effort at all.

Chapter Nine

Aching Bones

He will wipe every tear from their eyes.
There will be no more death or mourning or crying or pain,
for the old order of things has passed away.

Revelation 21:4 NIV

Marie hurt every day of her life. She'd been in a serious car wreck as a young woman many years before. The collision broke her hip and pulled it from the socket. Her pelvic bone had also been broken in the crash. The doctor's predictions were discouraging. They said she'd soon have arthritis and would require a hip replacement within several years.

But God answered her family's prayers, and she'd made it for a long period of time without either the arthritis or the hip replacement.

Then she had a fall where she fractured her spine. She'd dealt with back issues since that time, and as she began to age, the arthritis in her hip and pelvic bone became severe and the need for a hip replacement arrived. The doctors wanted to wait a few more years, so they sent her for pool therapy.

Marie was skeptical at first, but the warm water had been wonderful to ease her pain. She continued with the pool exercises for several months. As she gained strength, her pain lessened.

Marie had started with a low current for her sessions but had worked her way to the point where the water was bubbling like it was boiling. She had to work hard to push against the current while she did her exercises—but one day she realized that she wasn't hurting the way she had before. Her hard work had been worth it.

Marie had physical aches, but many of us also have heartaches. They usually aren't visible but you might have carried some of them since you were a child. Horrible things that others have done to you. Mistakes you've made that you can't get over. Scars from your past that cripple you. Fears and situations that you can't control.

That's when Dr. Jesus sends you for therapy in his Word. Immerse yourself in his promises. Soak in his words of forgiveness and healing. Turn up the current in your prayer life. And as time goes by, you'll discover that those heartaches have lessened, and you've become a stronger person of faith.

Father, the heartaches of life have caused me pain that hurts as much or more than physical pain. Nobody can see the pain in my heart, but I sure know it's there. How do I forgive those who scarred my childhood? How do I forgive myself for stupid things I've done that have hurt others? How do I get over the situations that have broken my heart and left me battered and broken? Remind me to dive into your Word to find the answers. Help me to soak in your forgiveness—even though I don't deserve it. Help me to spend more time in prayer because that's where I'll gain strength and relief from stress. Thank you for always having the answers to all that I need.

Why are you often so hesitant to seek the soul therapy that you need? Why is it important for you to get past those old things in your life?

Aquatic therapy, or pool therapy, consists of an exercise program that is performed in the water. It is a beneficial form of therapy that is useful for a variety of medical conditions. Aquatic therapy uses the physical properties of water to assist in patient healing and exercise performance.

CHAPTER TEN

Sweet Dreams

Fully awake, he rebuked the storm and shouted to the sea, "Hush!
Calm down!" All at once the wind stopped howling
and the water became perfectly calm.

MARK 4:39 TPT

The wind picked up and seemed to come from all
directions. The boat began to rock side to side and pitch
forward and back. Lightening lit the pitch-black sky, thunder
rumbled, and rain pelted. The disciples should've been
sleeping. It had been a stressful day of ministry by the lake
with Jesus. Yet the disciples couldn't sleep, not with the
storm raging all around them. In fact, they were so anxious
about the weather that they actually thought they might
lose their lives that night. I suspect we'd have reacted
exactly the same way.

Stressful situations and events can cause temporary
insomnia. The disciples worried about a violent storm and
couldn't close their eyes. We can also worry about storms
in our lives—sick children, a troubled marriage, financial

difficulties, an aging parent, infertility, selling a house, and so much more. Life can be hard.

The disciples had no need to fear the storm—they had Jesus right by their side. Jesus slept soundly, knowing that his Father in heaven had everything under control. Because, thankfully for us, he who watches over us neither slumbers nor sleeps. Aren't you thrilled to know that God never sleeps?

Friends, sleep is important to our bodies for obvious reasons, but because lack of sleep can create anxiety, and anxiety can lead to lack of sleep, we need to be careful not to fall into a vicious cycle, with one begetting the other.

Troubles may surround us, but Jesus never leaves us nor forsakes us. He is right by our side. He can calm our anxiousness and allay our fears. God is completely aware of the storms of life that stress and trouble us. He knows and he cares.

Let's pray tonight as we slip into a bubble bath that God will calm our storms. Once we've placed those cares in his hands, we need to let go of the worries. It's easier said than done, but he promises to take care of them for us.

Let the stresses drain away with the bathwater and have a sweet, stress-free night of rest.

Dear God, I know that rest and relaxation are important for my mental health and physical well-being, but sometimes the storms of life make me toss and turn just like that boat that held the disciples. Father, remind me often that you are always with me, that you comfort me, and that you have me in the palm of your hand—so what could I fear? Take away any anxious thoughts tonight and calm my soul with your presence. May I rest in your arms tonight, sweet heavenly Father, just as newborns do in their parents' loving embrace. Thank you, God, for rest that rejuvenates and refreshes. I love you, Lord.

Why do you toss and turn when the storms of life arrive? Why do you still worry even though Jesus is there with you?

That beautiful body of water called the Sea of Galilee is known for sudden, violent storms. At least four of the disciples were fishermen and should have been well-versed with the Sea of Galilee's spontaneous squalls. Yet, the disciples were terrified. Most likely that storm was unlike any other they'd faced as fishermen.

CHAPTER ELEVEN

Calming Splashes

The raging waves lifted themselves over and over,
high above the ocean's depths, letting out their mighty roar!
Yet at the sound of your voice they were all stilled by your might.
What a majestic King, filled with power!

PSALM 93:4-5 TPT

Have you ever been so stressed that it almost felt like your body was vibrating? Your stomach flipped and flopped with nerves. Your cheeks were red. It's for sure your blood pressure was up. You didn't even need to check it to know that. And your last good nerve was on display so everyone could step on it...and they did.

That perfectly described Debbie's day. There was just so much stuff to do—and not enough of her to do it. She was so stressed out that even she was worried about herself. Ready to mark one more thing off her 14-foot-long to-do list, she drove into the parking lot of the post office and pulled into one of the spaces that faced the river behind the building.

She was too worn out to walk into the post office, so she rolled the windows down and laid her head on the steering wheel. And that's when she noticed the whoosh of the water as it splashed upon the large rocks in the middle of the river and then headed downstream. It was faster than normal due to the fierce storm that had blown through earlier that morning.

Whoosh! Whooooosh! Whoosh! Gurgle. Whoosh! Whooooosh! Whoosh!

She sat there for about fifteen minutes, just listening to and watching the river. And you know what? She could feel the stress draining from her body as she enjoyed God's handiwork, as the soothing sound of the water eased the tension from her shoulders. Her headache began to ease, and her blood pressure started to stabilize.

Then she bowed her head, reminded of the verse that talks about how the sound of God's voice stills the raging waters. Reminded of what a mighty God he is. Debbie praised him—not just for how he could calm the waves, but for how he could also calm his child through the soothing sound of those waves.

A different woman left the parking lot that day. A woman who'd had calming splashes of Jesus that completely turned her day around.

Dear Jesus, I so often keep my eyes on my problems—on my stress-filled days—instead of keeping my eyes on you. When the storms of life come my way, remind me to go to the one who is mightier than the storm. Instead of focusing on my stress, remind me to focus on you. Lord, you know me so well. I'm grateful for the soothing sound of the water you've made, and for how that soothes my soul. And I'm thankful that not only can you calm the raging water, but you can calm me when I feel like the waves of life are about to overcome me. You're a mighty God and I love you.

Why do you think the sound of water is calming? How do those waters reflect God's mighty power?

You know that feeling of clear-headed calm that washes over you when you listen to water babbling down a stream? Researchers say they've pinpointed a scientific explanation for why sounds from nature have such a restorative effect on our psyche. According to a new study, they physically alter the connections in our brains, reducing our body's natural fight-or-flight instinct.

CHAPTER TWELVE

No Fractures Allowed

Seek the LORD and his strength;
seek his presence continually!

1 CHRONICLES 16:11 ESV

Becky was looking forward to attending the military ball with her husband. His deployment would end just in time, but she had so much to do before he returned. She ordered the sequined, red dress two sizes smaller than she normally wore. "I've got plenty of time to lose the weight," Becky decided. "I'll start jogging again next week."

One week into her jogging routine, she developed sharp, shooting pains in her right foot. A doctor confirmed her fears. "You have a stress fracture," Dr. Kevin said. "It's just a tiny crack and will heal on its own, but you're going to have to ice it, elevate your foot, and stay off of it for a bit." Wearing that two-sizes-too-small sequined red dress wasn't going to happen.

Becky sheepishly admitted that she'd taken shortcuts in

hopes to lose weight quickly. She never took time to stretch out, and she pushed herself too hard initially.

Which reminded her that she'd actually taken a lot of shortcuts lately—she'd cut her prayer time short each morning to work on spring cleaning projects before her husband returned. She still read her Bible, but just one or two verses a day and then worked on those income tax papers that she'd not finished. She'd stopped volunteering in the nursery on Sunday mornings, with the promise to herself that she'd return after her husband got home.

And she even stopped her bubble baths at night, which is where she spent quiet time thinking about all the blessings God had given her that day.

Becky realized she was causing a stress-fracture in her heart with all those shortcuts. And she knew just what she needed to repair the damage of a fractured relationship with God.

Friends, there are no shortcuts to an intimate relationship with God. We have to spend time with him in prayer, in his Word, and in our thoughts. And we especially need a relationship with him that's not fractured when we're facing a big event like a military deployment, new job, marriage, new baby, or other big life change.

Dear God, sometimes it's easy to slowly pull away from you when I get really busy and stressed. "I'll just skip this one day of Bible study," I tell myself. Or, "I'll pray quickly today, but longer tomorrow." But I know those shortcuts lead me on a path that just keeps getting farther and farther from you. When I'm busiest or most stressed, that's when my need for you is so great that I don't need to take any shortcuts at all. In fact, that's when I need more time with you, God. Help me to recognize my need for you during those times. Father, I don't ever want a fractured relationship with you.

Why is it so easy to skip time with God when you're really busy? Try to imagine your best friend cancelling time with you at the last minute because they're just too busy. How would you feel?

Being busy is an addiction and it can be as challenging to stop as other addictions such as alcohol, shopping, or working because it is a way to escape or numb yourself. But, unlike other addictions, Western society puts a high value on being busy. We are conditioned to believe that being busy equates to being good, worthy, and successful.

CHAPTER THIRTEEN

Beside Still Waters

The LORD is my shepherd; I shall not want.
He makes me lie down in green pastures.
He leads me beside still waters.
He restores my soul.

PSALM 23:1–3 ESV

We're all familiar with Psalm 23. Those words are often used at funerals. They're featured on greeting cards and artwork. But have you ever wondered about those words *still waters* and why God uses still waters in this chapter that he wrote to comfort us?

Have you ever been by a quiet stream? The surface is so clear it's like a mirror. It reflects the peaceful beauty of God's creation. The water draws us to it and the silence and stillness invite us to also be motionless. Those still waters give us rest for our soul. Scientists say the sound of water even has a positive effect on our brains.

Can you think of anything that a stressed and grieving person could use more than calmness and restful silence? God knows what we need to restore our souls, to refresh us in our heartache. But it's hard to hear his words of comfort if we're zipping around, or if we're in turmoil and constant action.

When we're still, we can hear God's soft whispers. We can draw close to the only one who can truly comfort an aching heart. After all, he grieved the loss of his beloved Son. Only someone who's walked the path of grief truly understands how we feel in our loss. And when God soothes our stress-filled soul, we won't lack for anything. He fills the empty places with his comfort as only he can.

Have you ever noticed the line "He leads me beside still waters" in these verses? He doesn't send us and our anxieties to the still waters alone. He is with us. Through every lonely night. Through every heartbroken day. Through those moments when tears overwhelm us. We don't have to go to the still waters alone, and we don't have to go through our grief alone. What a beautiful picture to imagine him holding our hand as he leads us to where we can find still waters to restore our hearts and souls.

Lord, I'm so grateful for the words of comfort you put in the Bible. I'm always amazed at how you've addressed every stressful situation I'll ever encounter. Grief is one of the hardest ones. It overwhelms my soul. It colors my days with darkness. It awakens me in the night and brings tears that leave me feeling empty and drained. Thank you for the promise of still waters and for the fact that you will lead me there. I'm not alone and never will be. You're a precious God and I don't know how I'd go through life without your presence and your comfort. Thank you, Lord, for always being all that I need in every situation.

Why do you think Psalm 23
is such a popular passage of Scripture?
How has it touched you personally?

Grief can be stressful and depleting. Emotionally, grief is a mixture of raw feelings such as sorrow, anguish, anger, regret, longing, fear, disappointment, blame, and deprivation. Grief experienced physically can be felt in forms of exhaustion, emptiness, tension, sleeplessness, and loss of appetite.

CHAPTER FOURTEEN

Sticky Situations

Do not be anxious about anything, but in every situation, by prayer and petition, with thanksgiving, present your requests to God. And the peace of God, which transcends all understanding, will guard your hearts and your minds in Christ Jesus.

PHILIPPIANS 4:6-7 NIV

"Look, Mommy, my dolphin is blowing bubbles!" Jan loved watching her daughter play in the bathtub, but she also anticipated her own bubble bath later that night, after all three kids were in bed. It had been a stressful evening: an afternoon tee-ball game for one child and a spelling bee for another. When Jan knelt near the tub to wash her daughter's long hair, her fingers snagged a tangle. It didn't take long to discover the source of it. "Yuck! Sweetie, you have gum stuck in your hair." *Well, there goes time for my bubble bath,* Jan thought, knowing it would take some time to detangle the mess.

Jan remembered giving her daughter a stick of gum earlier, but she couldn't remember when. Jan kept gum in her purse, because she knew it was a quick stress-reliever when she was really anxious. And tee-ball games and spelling bees made her anxious. She didn't know if she got more nervous for her kids or herself. She just knew those situations made her anxious, even though she enjoyed the activities.

Oh, she made sure to pray. She knew that was the best solution to her anxiety, and she always prayed with her kids before all of their big events and each morning before school. But sometimes she just needed an immediate stress reliever, and gum seemed to work.

Jan knows that chewing gum, though certainly not a permanent fix to worries, can actually reduce anxiety and stress because the act of chewing reduces the stress hormone, cortisol. And she also knows that God has a permanent fix. That doesn't mean we won't have problems in this world—the Bible tells us we will. But God wants us to exchange our burdens and cares for his peace. He promises us that he'll do that for us and take away our stress.

Memorize Philippians 4:6-7 and trust God with that permanent fix. Stick a pack of gum in your purse for a quick fix, but just be sure to keep it out of a little darling's hair.

Dear God, I know from your Word that as long as I am in this world, I will have troubles and stress. Sometimes, the troubles will have an easy solution, and sometimes the difficulties will be hard-pressed for answers. But, God, I also know that rather than a quick fix to my problems, I need to learn to turn every situation over to you and leave it in your hands. Once I've placed it in your hands, help me to leave it there. Help me to feel your presence during my anxious times, like spelling bees, ball games, piano recitals, jury duty, or doctor appointments. Comfort me and remind me that there is nothing too big that you can't handle.

Is it difficult for you to give God a problem and then leave it in his hands? What situation do you need to present to God?

Munching on crunchy vegetables or fruits, like carrots, celery, or apples can help you relax because the crunching helps relieve jaw tension, an area of the body where stress can build up.

Chapter Fifteen

Showers of Blessings

"Fear not, for I am with you;
be not dismayed, for I am your God;
I will strengthen you, I will help you,
I will uphold you with my righteous right hand."

Isaiah 41:10 esv

Jill's newborn son, Adam, was beautiful. But as the months went by, he started missing milestones that babies are supposed to reach at various ages. It soon became clear Adam would never talk, sit up, or walk.

More children joined their family. Children with no health issues. Jill loved them all, with a tender love for the little son who required extra care. Her heart and days were full.

Jill tended Adam's feeding tube. She performed numerous medical procedures for him every day, carrying her son from place to place. She sat and stroked his hair and told him how much she loved him. Jill was up many times during the night as medical equipment beeped warnings. Her days were beyond full. She did it all while she still cared for the needs of the rest of her family, doing the laundry, cooking dinner, cleaning the house, and playing with her children. But she did it all with love.

Jill didn't begrudge a minute of all the care she gave, but she was beyond exhausted. Some days her stress levels left her feeling like a rubber band that had been stretched to the limits—like she'd snap from the stress at any time. Her back and body ached, and her limbs were tired.

There was certainly no time for a bubble bath for Jill. She did well to get a five-minute shower each day. Many women would have folded under all the stress and physical demands. But not Jill.

You see, Jill had discovered the best place to get the strength she needed. She didn't have time to sit down to read, so she played an audio Bible, the promises from God's Word soaking into her weary soul. She prayed as she folded laundry. And she played praise and worship music. The precious words of the songs showered her with blessings as they told about God's power and comfort, and how he's always with us.

Do you feel like that stretched rubber band? Go to the source where Jill found her strength. Showers of blessings are waiting for you there.

Father, sometimes you ask me to do things that are difficult for me, that wipe me out physically, that defeat me emotionally, and even impact me spiritually. Some days I feel as if I can't do it another day, that I can't take the stress and the mental burden. But I know my strength is in you. Remind me of how—even in the difficult times—you've still showered me with blessings. I want to finish strong for you, Lord, and for my family. Give me the strength and courage to do that because I know I can't do it under my own strength. Refresh me as if I've had a long bubble bath and help me to keep on keeping on.

Why do you think God sometimes asks
you to carry heavy loads in your life?
How can you discover showers
of blessings in those moments?

Between 40 to 70% of caregivers suffer from
depression, while many caregivers have anxiety
as a result of the stress associated with providing
care. Anger and irritability are also common
symptoms of caregiver stress syndrome. The
chronic stress may lead to high blood pressure,
diabetes, and a compromised immune system.

yummy Goodness

Do not forget to do good and to share with others,
for with such sacrifices God is pleased.

HEBREWS 13:16 NIV

Pie therapy exists. We often talk about stress-eating, but an even better concept is a little newer: stress-baking. Psychologists agree that baking is a form of creative expression, just like other artistic endeavors, and it gives people an outlet that reduces stress—with the side benefit that it produces something that will taste good.

Baking is therapeutic because it typically keeps the creative chef focused on exact measurements and precise steps of completion. Focusing on a recipe, and not the long, stressful day you've had, can distract your thoughts, giving your brain a much-needed break from anxiety.

What works even better to conquer stress is to double up on the recipe and share the final product with someone else. That feeling of serving others, of comforting another person who might be going through a difficult time, can have a healing effect on our stress levels too. In his Word, God asks us to take care of others. We can be the hands and feet of Jesus by whipping up something yummy in the kitchen.

What's on the menu? A double batch of soup, one for your family and one for the sick friend down the street? Two casseroles, one for dinner and one for the new mom in your small group? One cake to eat, and one cake to share with a grieving widow? What about a double batch of cookies, some for your family, and some to share with the teachers?

At night after you've finished having fun with your stress-baking and cooking for others, soak in a warm bubble bath and pray for each of the folks who will receive your containers filled with love and delicious food. They might be going through anxious times, and you might be the only one praying for them.

Cooking and baking offers comfort to the chef who's otherwise stressed with work, family, commitments, and church. When that chef takes the time to unwind in the kitchen, and at the same time pleases God by baking goodies for someone in need, then it's a win-win all the way around.

Dear God, thank you for your provisions. Thank you for yummy food and for the joy that I feel when I prepare something in the kitchen—especially if I prepare something to share with a friend. God, when life gets tough and I am stressed, thank you for the distraction of creating in the kitchen. Help me to be mindful of others who might need a special homemade treat that will remind them they're not alone or forgotten and that you care about and love them. God, as I measure in the kitchen, help me to remember that no one can measure how wide and long and high and deep is your love.

Does cooking relax you? Who in your circle of family and friends needs to be reminded of the love of Jesus? How can you share that when you drop off a casserole or dessert this week?

There is talk about a new trend of using cooking classes to treat mental health disorders. You don't need to have a disorder to benefit. Instead of viewing cooking as a chore, use it as a way to relax at the end of the day.

CHAPTER SEVENTEEN

Fighting Gloves

Be angry and do not sin;
do not let the sun go down on your anger.

EPHESIANS 4:26 ESV

Cindy and Brad had a humdinger of an argument one night after dinner. The husband and wife usually got along well, but both of them were under a lot of stress with their jobs. Brad said something that Cindy wouldn't have even thought twice about under other circumstances, but on that night, it struck the wrong nerve and the conversation took a nosedive. And became louder. And meaner, as both said hateful things to hurt the other. By the time bedtime rolled around, the atmosphere was cold enough to make ice cubes in the room, neither was speaking to the other, and Brad went to bed in the guest room.

Whew, there's nothing like an argument with your spouse (or any loved one) to ratchet up the stress level, is there? Often there are tears, usually way more than are warranted, and at times with a self-righteous, "How dare he speak to me like that."

As Cindy sat in a bubble bath that night trying to ease the stress—and wiping tears—a nudge of conviction slowly kicked in for the hateful things she'd said. She knew the only answer to get rid of her stress was to ask forgiveness for hurting the one she loved, and for damaging a precious relationship that God had put together.

That's why God says not to let the sun go down on our wrath. He knows it's not good for our physical bodies or for our spiritual well-being when we're at odds with each other.

But we're often slow learners, aren't we?

Those moments when the fighting gloves have caused our stress levels to rise are the perfect time to tell God we're sorry and then go to our loved one and sincerely apologize. A mended relationship is the perfect stress-reliever and the remainder of the day or night will be sweet instead of filled with sour grapes.

Is there a relationship you need to mend? Maybe you need a bubble bath and a nudge of conviction. Don't let the sun go down with unresolved anger. It's great advice.

Lord, it's funny how stress can cause even more stress. I love my family and friends, but when I'm under a lot of stress I'm often thoughtless and unkind. I snap at those close to me. I say ugly things. And I have no patience with anyone. I know that's not pleasing to you and that it will lead to fractured relationships if it continues. Help me to discover the sources of my stress, to fix what can be fixed, and to turn the rest over to you. Give me a heart that responds with kindness. Give me a tongue that speaks with love. Help me to cherish the precious relationships you've given me.

How can stress damage and change your relationships? Why do you think God says not to let the sun go down on your anger?

According to the American Institute of Stress, more than a quarter of people surveyed in 2014 felt alienated from a friend or family member because of stress, and over half had fought with people close to them because of it.

CHAPTER EIGHTEEN

Hobbies

Honor her for all that her hands have done,
and let her works bring her praise at the city gate.

PROVERBS 31:31 NIV

Have you heard of Grandma Moses? She's the internationally known painter who exhibited her first piece of artwork when she was 78 years old. Anna Mary Robertson Moses, born in 1860, worked on a farm almost her entire life, raising five children, crops, and livestock. Caring for those humans and animals and laboring in the fields all day had to lead to a stress-filled life for Mrs. Moses. And, it's doubtful that bubble baths were part of her routine.

Somehow, Mrs. Moses found time to craft beautiful needlework pictures and quilts. What a stress-reliever it must've been to sit quietly in the evening and enjoy her hobby.

When arthritis halted her needlework, Mrs. Moses, in her late seventies, found that she could paint the same farm scenes she'd been crafting. A newspaper reviewer dubbed her "Grandma Moses," and the name stuck. The self-taught artist exhibited her work into her 90s and continued to paint until just weeks before her death at the age of 101.

God gave Grandma Moses many talents. Cooking, baking, gardening, raising livestock, crafting, painting, and probably others. What talents has God given you? Have you ever thought about using your hobby as a stress-reliever? Studies show that engaging in hobby activities for at least twenty minutes a week prevents fatigue and encourages better physical health. God knew our hobbies could calm our anxious minds.

Hobbies provide a stress-free break, recharging us by doing something we enjoy and making us better able to handle the responsibilities of family and work. A hobby serves to still our minds from a frantic schedule or to-do list and lets us work with our hands to create something special, something meaningful.

God gives us talents as personal gifts and blessings, but he also wants us to use those talents to bless others. Thank God for the talents he's given you and ask him to reveal ways that your hobby can ease your stressed mind after a long day. Then ask him who you can share some of your finished projects with—possibly someone who is going through an especially challenging time.

Dear God, thank you for the talents you've given me, those that I might have already explored and those that I might not have explored just yet. Help me to find ways to use my hands in worthy, creative ways: to still my mind when I am stressed and anxious about everything on my to-do list. Thank you for that feeling of accomplishment when I've used my hands for something constructive with the talents you've given me. Please help my hobbies and activities to put my mind at ease and turn my thoughts to you. And God, it would be a special treat if I could bless someone else with my hobby. Please show me someone to share a finished project with.

In what ways do your hobbies relax you?
How do you know your talents come from
God? How does that encourage you to
share your talents with others?

According to positive psychology, a fairly new
branch of psychology that focuses on what makes
life worthwhile, gratifications is a term that
means the important activities that bring meaning
and pleasure to life. Gratifications reduces stress,
and hobbies are an example of such.

CHAPTER NINETEEN

Orange Fresh

The Lord is good to those who wait for him,
to the soul who seeks him.

LAMENTATIONS 3:25 ESV

Rachel zipped around the house like a long-tailed cat in a room full of rocking chairs. She was having what she called a "Domino Day." That's where her day was so stacked with appointments that if there were a glitch, her day would collapse like a Domino display gone bad. She seemed to have a lot of those stressful days, times when she desperately needed a bubble bath.

Rachel knew that if she started the day late, she'd have a major mess, so she was determined to be on time. She figured she could save a few minutes by not washing her hair and using dry shampoo to freshen it. Dashing into the bathroom, she grabbed the can of dry shampoo from the sink top and sprayed her hair liberally.

And that's when she noticed that she smelled oranges. Her jaw dropped as it dawned on her what she'd done. She'd sprayed her hair with air freshener instead of dry shampoo. There was no way she had time to wash her hair, so she guessed she'd just go through her day smelling like a basket of oranges.

We can do some stupid stuff when we're stressed and rushing, can't we? That's why God says waiting on him and seeking him is a good thing. All of us will have busy stressful days, but Rachel had a plethora of them because she didn't have patience to wait on God, and she said yes to things way too often without seeking God's guidance before she took on new responsibilities.

There are consequences when we don't seek God's guidance and when we don't wait on him. We end up overscheduled and stressed. That creates tension in our relationships. We reach the point where we can't do it all, and then we add guilt to the mix because we're women and we somehow have the misguided notion that we can do *everything* and do it well. As Rachel learned, it's always better to seek God—because otherwise, you just might spend your day smelling like oranges.

Father, I sure can get myself in messes, can't I? You made me, so you know I'm often impulsive. Someone will ask me to do something, and I take on a new task without seeking you for wisdom first. And then I'm stressed because I have too much to do. I've dug myself into giant holes so many times that you'd think I'd learn my lesson, but evidently I'm a slow learner. So, Lord, teach me to come to you first to seek your will for me. Help me to wait on you, knowing that you have my best interests at heart. Remind me that it's so much easier to wait for a message from you than it is to clean up the messes of my hasty decisions.

What's the craziest thing you've
done when you've been stressed and
overwhelmed? How does it make a
difference to wait on God when it comes
to your schedule?

You can effectively manage being busy for
significant periods of time without a negative
impact. But when you are overscheduled, you can
only continue at this speed for a period of time
before the negative impacts of stress
and anxiety kick in.

CHAPTER TWENTY

Murky Waters

Let's not get tired of doing what is good.
At just the right time we will reap
a harvest of blessing if we don't give up.

GALATIANS 6:9 NLT

"Don't throw the baby out with the bathwater." Don't
you think that's a silly phrase? The tall tale that goes with
the saying, though it's not completely proven true, is that in
the 1500s, baths consisted of a tub filled with warm water,
and the first person to have the pleasure of bathing was the
man of the house. Next came all the sons in the household,
followed by the women and children. Supposedly, the water
became so clouded and filthy that the baby could get lost in
the murky waters. Apparently a German proverb, the saying
warns of disposing of something important while discarding
the unimportant.

Sometimes we get lost in the murky waters of our busy
schedules. We allow our days to fill up with way more tasks
than anyone could ever accomplish. And then when we're

drowning in all the details, the first thing we toss from our list is our devotional time with God. We make excuses that we'll catch up tomorrow...or next week. We toss out our precious time with the Lord, and then we wonder why we're stressed and anxious.

Friends, time with God is what we should hang onto with the tightest grip. We don't want that to slip from our grasp, ever. Make daily quiet time with God a priority and ask him to help everything else fall into place. Rank your to-do list and march on. You may have to put some things of lesser importance aside until another day or ask for help from someone else to accomplish those tasks.

Life is hard and stressful at times. But God is good and he wants to lighten our load and help us get through each day, one day at a time. God is our ever-present help in times of stress.

Don't toss out everything just because the water of life gets a little murky. Say a prayer, hang onto the baby, take a deep breath, and press on. Jesus has this and all the other details of your life.

Dear God, sometimes I feel like the waters of life around me are so murky that I couldn't find my way out, no matter how hard I paddled. At times, I just want to give up, to not even try, to accept defeat and quit. But, I don't want to be a quitter. I want to honor my commitments and carry out my responsibilities— but I also need to get rid of this stress. If I need to delegate some of my duties, help me to recognize that. Please give me the strength each day to get through my tasks at hand. And no matter how murky the waters, God, please help me to see you clearly and keep my focus on you.

Have you experienced a time where you felt like giving up? How did God pull you through that stressful time? How can you trust God to be with you when the waters of life seem murky?

Though research has shown that stress can have negative consequences on a person's life, stress may actually help one advance in his or her spiritual walk. Faith can also positively affect stress and help a person to cope.

When Life Is Hard

My health may fail, and my spirit may grow weak,
but God remains the strength of my heart;
he is mine forever.

PSALM 73:26 NLT

Ken's cancer diagnosis devastated his family. Surgery would be performed in two days. The family was reeling from the news when tragedy struck again. Ken's wife, Sarah, went to the doctor for possible pneumonia. Several tests later, she sat dumbstruck, having also received a cancer diagnosis. As she prepared to leave, the doctor said, "My office will call you to set up an appointment with the surgeon." Talk about stress.

What were the odds of two family members being diagnosed with cancer in a 48-hour time period? How would she tell her family when they were already so upset over Ken's cancer and upcoming surgery? She felt numb as she drove home. All she wanted was to go home, sink into a hot bubble bath, and pretend this week had never happened.

She started the hot water, poured some bubble bath in, and settled into the warmth. Thankfully, Ken was gone for several hours, but she knew she had to decide how to tell him when he got home, because he'd want to know what the doctor said. And then they'd have to talk about how they were going to tell their children and grandchildren.

This wasn't fair. Life wasn't supposed to be filled with stress like this. It was just too hard. How would they care for each other with both of them dealing with cancer at the same time? Sarah would have cried, but the pain was too deep for tears.

Sarah did what she'd done with every other hard situation in her life. "God, I don't know what to do. I'm worried about both of us. I don't know how we're going to get through this. But you've been faithful to us through every trial. As our pastor says, 'Even when I can't track you, I can trust you.' This is too big for me, so I'm placing us in your hands, knowing that nothing can happen to us without coming through you first."

Are you in a situation where your health is failing and you're anxious? Even when you can't track what God is doing, you can still trust him.

Father, whether my health fails or my spirit is weak, I'm never alone for you promise to be with me and to be the strength of my heart. I'm so grateful that whenever life's hardships are too big for me, they're never too big for you. I couldn't make it through life without you. You've always provided what I needed in the past and I'm going to trust you for that in the future. Give me the strength I need to go through this trial and help me to learn what you want me to through this. Then after the trial is past, help me to use what I've been through to comfort others who are going through difficult times.

How do you react when you face problems
that seem too big for you? How has God
helped you through anxious moments
in the past?

Any type of major illness is a significant stressor
for the entire family. One person being ill does
not just affect that person but everyone around
them. A major illness is one of the worst stressors
we can endure as it can go on for years, taking its
emotional toll on everyone.

CHAPTER TWENTY-TWO

Take the Plunge

You will show me the way of life,
granting me the joy of your presence
and the pleasures of living with you forever.

PSALM 16:11 NLT

Daredevil divers plunge from cliffs one-hundred-thirty-five feet high into the gurgling warm seas of the Pacific Ocean in Acapulco, Mexico. It's like a giant bubble bath when they land in the frothy warm water, but what a scary leap before that. Can you imagine the rapid heartbeat of these divers just before taking that daring jump?

That rapid heartbeat, however, is a result of a positive stress, called "eustress." Eustress is beneficial or good stress that produces positive feelings about life. It results in increased motivation, satisfaction, fulfillment, and excitement.

If you need good stress, why not try a new adventure? Maybe it won't be diving from a cliff into a gigantic bubble-bath, but if it's new to you, it's certainly an adventure. You might try something as simple as reading a book in a new genre or learning how to decorate a cake. Or you might decide to try rock climbing or even take a sky diving class.

God promises to be with us during our challenging and stressful times, but he'll also accompany us on those exhilarating and fun adventures too. After all, God is the creator of everything. That means he made those exciting adventures. Sometimes we're guilty of thinking of God as a problem-solver, the amazing Savior of the world—which he is—but maybe we haven't ever viewed him as the life of the party.

God gives life and he promises it abundantly. Our walk with him should be an adventure every single day—one where stress and anxiety disappear. The greatest adventure of all times is walking with Jesus. It doesn't get any more exciting than the joy of his presence and the pleasure of eternal life with him.

Treat every day as a new adventure in your walk with the Lord. Remember that Jesus is with you wherever you go, and then dive in. Take the plunge.

Dear God, I love you passionately and recognize you as Lord and Savior of my life, but I sometimes see you as a somber God carrying the weight of the world. I think I'm doing that because I often feel like I have the weight of the world on my shoulders, like life is getting me down. When I'm stressed to the max, remind me first and foremost that you are my greatest adventure. Remind me that life can't get more adventurous than a daily walk with you and the promise of life eternal. Lord, you are the author and creator of adventure and fun and excitement. Help me to live every day in that joyful mindset.

How can a new adventure take away
the stress of a long day? What are some
of the fun adventures God has allowed
you to have?

Adventure sports are one of the most effective
ways to release stress. It helps you release pent-up
tension and replaces it with euphoria and energy.
Taking part in any number of adventure-related
activities gives a sense of accomplishment
and confidence.

CHAPTER TWENTY-THREE

What Now

I was once young, but now I'm old.
Not once have I found a lover of God forsaken by him,
nor have any of their children gone hungry.

PSALM 37:25 TPT

Debbie had always wanted to get married, but that hadn't worked out. There were benefits of being single though. She had time with her girlfriends, traveled to exotic locales, and she had a great career. Debbie made a six-figure salary, had her healthcare covered, received retirement benefits, and drove a nice company car.

She'd bought a house and furnished it. Her closets were crammed with fashionable clothes, rows of cute shoes, and a collection of designer handbags. Life was comfortable, and she'd settled into an easy and secure lifestyle.

But then she started hearing rumblings at work that there were problems with the company. She watched as several co-workers had their jobs terminated. A few weeks later, the moment she'd dreaded arrived. Debbie received a pink slip letting her know that she was no longer an employee of the company. Effective immediately.

Carrying the box with the personal items from her office, she got her keys out to drive home, and then realized that she'd no longer have the use of the company car. Her mom came and drove her home.

As months went by without finding a new job, Debbie began to stress more and more. Her savings were dwindling, but the bills were still coming in each month. She economized every way she could, but circumstances were getting serious.

Bubble baths were one of the few little luxuries she still had left. But she was too stressed for them to be enjoyable as they once were. As she hunkered down in the water, she yelled out at God, "I feel so alone. Don't you care?"

Then she heard God's whispers to her soul, "Of course I do. I will take care of you. Have you ever seen the words, 'And then God failed me' in the Bible? I've never failed my children in the past, and I never will."

Even though the situation wasn't better, just remembering that God had cared for her in the past, and would continue to do so in the future, was enough.

God will do the same for you no matter where you are in life right now.

Father, losing a job is scary. It feels awful being unemployed. Security disappears, but the bills don't. I worry about how to pay the bills, how to buy food, and what to do for health insurance. You promised to take care of me, and I'm holding you to that. If you care enough to feed the birds, then I know that you'll provide food for me as well. I will trust you in the stressful interim. Thank you for always being a faithful God. I know that your promises are true. I don't ever want to take that for granted.

Why does losing a job provide so much stress? What lessons can be learned about trusting God during those times?

Our jobs are much more than just the way we make a living. They influence how we see ourselves, as well as the way others see us. They give us structure, purpose, and meaning. That's why job loss and unemployment can be so stressful.

CHAPTER TWENTY-FOUR

In the Storm

I prayed to the LORD, and he answered me.
He freed me from all my fears.

PSALM 34:4 NLT

Traveling from San Francisco to Georgia, Mary Beth's adult son encountered a sudden snowstorm late one evening. The Southern native needed to hear the voice of his mom during the harrowing drive. She tried her best to calm her son, though it was all she could do to hide her own panic. Not surprisingly, the calls often dropped with lack of service, sometimes after he'd uttered words like, "I can't see anything in front of me but the lights of the eighteen-wheeler. I'm starting to slide. I can't...." *Silence.*

Thousands of miles away, Mary Beth struggled to allay her anxious thoughts. Everything imaginable popped into her head during the silence between phone calls. She knew what she had to do. It was all that she could do. Mary Beth reached out to a few dear friends and prayer warriors that she knew were still awake and asked them to pray for her son's safety. Then she ran the water for a bubble bath, sunk deep into the warmth of the water, and prayed.

And prayed. And prayed. Until hours later, when her son called from a hotel room, safe, but exhausted. "I'm taking a warm shower, then going to sleep," he said. "I'll wait out the storm and travel later."

Fearful thoughts about our children or other family members cause such anxiety, don't they? God doesn't want us to be afraid. He says so many times in the Bible, repeating the words, "Fear not."

That's easier said than done, isn't it? But he means it. God's promises are true. We can trust God to remove our fears. We can trust his goodness and know that he has plans for our good, and that means plans for our children and family members too. God loves our children infinitely more than we can imagine and he's going to protect and take care of those we love.

When you're afraid, pray. Give God the situation and your fears, and then trust him to take care of the rest. He can handle it all.

Father, sometimes my anxieties take me captive and I tremble with worry and doubt. Will my husband be safe in his job? Are my children protected from evil? Can I keep up with the bills this month? And, sometimes, my fears get so strong that they hold me back. I keep them in the forefront of my mind instead of putting you there, and I miss the joys of life with you. Allay my fears. Help me to let go of the things that stress me out and help me to give them all to you. Help me to live a life of joy, free from the worries of this world, because you promise to be with me always. Thank you, God, for that promise.

Think of a time when you were frightened.
What insight can you gain from that
situation that can grow your trust in God?

The fight-or-flight response is a physiological reaction that results from a particularly scary or frightening situation. The situation can take place mentally or physically. The response triggers the release of hormones that enable you to flee the situation and run to safety or stand boldly and deal with the threat.

CHAPTER TWENTY-FIVE

Moving On

"Have I not commanded you? Be strong and courageous.
Do not be frightened, and do not be dismayed,
for the LORD your God is with you wherever you go."

JOSHUA 1:9 ESV

Kathy's bubble bath wasn't relaxing her like it normally did. That's because she was crying ugly tears while she soaked. Her face was blotched and red from where she'd cried so long and so hard. "What's wrong?" her husband asked as he walked into the bathroom.

She finally choked out, "It's the move."

He said, "I thought you were excited about my new job and moving to the new house." Real estate was cheaper in the area where they were moving and he was getting a housing allowance at this new job, so they would have a gorgeous and much bigger home when they moved.

"I am, but it's ten hours away from here and we won't know anybody. I'm going to miss our church and all our friends and neighbors here, and it's going to be sad leaving behind all the memories we've made in this house."

Change is often good, but it's still hard, isn't it? It can be a fear-laced stress with unique layers of anxiety. Whether it's a new job, a new church, a new home, or even a new spouse, it's difficult to let go of the past or the comfort of where we are now and run off to a new and uncertain future. It feels like being a new kid in the middle of the school year, standing awkwardly on the classroom threshold.

Moving is one of the top five stressors, but any change can be stressful. Sometimes it's stepping out in faith for the big dream God has given you. Maybe it's taking in foster children even though you feel inadequate to help them. Perhaps it's taking on a leadership role in a ministry even though your favorite place is in the back row or hiding behind a potted plant.

Whatever our "new" is, God has given us a precious promise: we don't need to be anxious. Instead, we can be strong and courageous. How? Because God promises to be with us wherever we go—and there's no better travel companion as we walk the pathways of life.

Lord, I'm facing some new situations in my life and that's left me feeling unsettled and anxious. I know you've opened these doors for me. I don't want to be stressed about this, but I am. I want to be strong and courageous for you. Thank you for the assurance that you will be with me wherever I go. That calms so many of my fears because I know whatever circumstance I'm in, I'll never be alone. As I step into new situations, help me touch the lives of others for you. Help me to be an encouragement and a blessing to all those I meet and help your sweetness shine from my life.

Why do you think moving causes so much stress? As you face new circumstances, what difference does it make to know that God will always be with you no matter where you go?

Excessive stress can make us pessimistic, causing us to lose focus on the task at hand and bog ourselves down in more stress. When you're moving, try to adopt a can-do attitude to help you through the tough parts. Focus on the positives, like meeting new people, exploring a new area, and finding fun activities to do in your new place.

CHAPTER TWENTY-SIX

Don't Strike Out

Know this, my beloved brothers:
let every person be quick to hear, slow to speak, slow to anger;
for the anger of man does not produce the righteousness of God.

JAMES 1:19-20 ESV

When the wandering Israelites ran out of water, they grumbled and quarreled and rose up against Moses and Aaron. Water was vitally important to them in the desert. The people were stressed. Aaron was anxious. And Moses was just plain exhausted from all the grumbling.

God's instructions to Moses were to "speak to the rock" and God would bring forth water. God planned a miracle, but Moses took matters into his own hands, or shall we say, staff.

Moses was stressed to the max with all the grumbling and complaining. He was worn out from all those responsibilities. Honestly, can you blame him? The Israelites were ungrateful, sinful, blinded-to-miracles troublemakers. Sort of sounds like a bunch of us God-followers today, right?

Moses didn't handle the stress well and chose

disobedience. Moses struck the rock with his staff after losing his cool with the people and calling them rebels. And he took credit for the water that gushed from the rock too.

God, in his love and mercy, gave the Israelites a bubbling, gurgling rush of refreshing water to nourish the people and livestock. And he told Moses that he wouldn't see the promised land because of his disobedience.

Friends, life is hard. Others around us grumble, exasperating us. Our families whine and complain, causing stress and annoyance. The boss is angry. The salesclerk is rude. The car breaks down. And the rain ruins a vacation. Life is tough. But God is good. God is always good.

We can't allow the actions of others to affect our own. Just think of all the times other people squabbling has led us to the edge. To allow ourselves to get so stressed that we are disobedient to God robs us of the joy he promises. When we get so stressed that we're tempted to sin, we can take a deep breath. Walk away for a second. Pray for a long time. Jump in a bubble bath. Be careful not to sin. God has way too many rebels. He could use some strong faith-filled followers.

God, please forgive me for my disobedience. Sometimes, it's easy to read about the Israelites and wonder how they could do what they did, but I'm guilty of the same doubts and failures. I'm quick to forget your miracles and then I grumble and complain when things don't go my way or when life seems difficult. Forgive me for the times I was so stressed I lost my temper and "struck the rock" like Moses did instead of being obedient to you. I don't want stress and anxiety to control my life. Your plan is always best. Help me to remember that and to keep my eyes open for those miracles, and freedom from stress, that come when I am obedient to you.

Does frustration reveal your true character or a completely different you? If your answer is the latter, how can you respond differently the next time you are stressed?

With 2.5 million Hebrews needing approximately 40 liters of water per day for basic survival, Moses would need to supply 100 million liters of water every day. Niagara Falls could supply the daily needs of the Israelites every 17 seconds.

CHAPTER TWENTY-SEVEN

At the Spa

Pour out all your worries and stress upon him
and leave them there, for he always tenderly cares for you.

1 Peter 5:7 tpt

Could you use a day at the spa? The Subterranean Spa at the Grove Park Inn in Asheville, North Carolina, is a 43,000-square-foot experience with twenty water features: rock walls, tunnels, waterfalls, underwater music, and cool lighting.

The day begins with a fluffy robe. Guests can enjoy hot tea by the firepit while covered with warm blankets. Shucks, it's relaxing just thinking about it. And then comes the hard part— deciding which of the soothing treatments you want first.

There are foot treatments with honey and oils for an hour of restful soaks. They offer facials that brighten and rejuvenate your skin. And, oh, the massages. Essential oils, aromatherapy, hot stones, and warm wraps promise deep relaxation and minds that are at rest.

A day of indulgence like this guarantees a soothing

atmosphere, and rest and relaxation for stressed bodies and minds. Unfortunately, many of us don't make time for ourselves like we should, and money is sometimes difficult to scrape together for extras.

Spa treatments can provide health benefits: cardiovascular regulation, better rest, lowered blood pressure, reduced stress and anxiety, and relief from aches and pains. Massages release serotonin—the happy hormone.

Did you know that there's an even better spa? God's spa for the soul. Make time to hang out there. The good news is that it's free. God begins by clothing us with righteousness and then detoxes our hearts to remove impurities. He gives us special times to be still and hang out with him, refreshing us as nothing else can do.

Are you stressed? Choose the treatment of God's Word. Soak in the sweet promises that you'll find there. Massage away your cares with time in prayer. The aches and pains of your soul will disappear. When you fill your heart with Jesus, your mind will be at rest. And you'll discover there's always an appointment available for you.

Father, I'm often stressed, and when I am, a day at the spa sounds wonderful for some rest and relaxation in a soothing environment. I'm so grateful that you have an even better spa—a spa for the soul where I can rest in your presence, where your Word eases the aches and pains that fill my heart, and where times in prayer massage away my cares no matter what circumstances I face. I don't know how I'd make it through life without the soothing power of your love. Thank you so much for paying the price with your life and for the assurance that an appointment with you is always available whenever I want to take advantage of it.

What do you most need from God's spa
for the soul? How does spending time with
him invigorate and refresh you?

Getting a massage is beneficial for more than just
relaxation. Massage is an effective type of therapy
for many different ailments. Headaches, arthritis,
back pain, injury recovery, and circulation can all
be aided by massage therapy.

CHAPTER TWENTY-EIGHT

Why Wait

Everything should be done in a fitting and orderly way.

1 CORINTHIANS 14:40 NIV

Benjamin Franklin once said, "Don't put off until tomorrow what you can do today." Though occasionally necessary, procrastination usually leads to bad results. Remember when you put off a big project until the last minute—an assignment at work, a ten-page paper in college, or planning a special event for someone? Does it make you anxious just thinking about that stress?

Procrastination can lead to a vicious cycle. When we're distracted by stress, it's easier to put things off. Then we worry about those things we've left undone. The more those things accumulate, the more overwhelmed we feel.

Let's not get into that cycle. Tonight, when you're filling the tub with bubbles—yes, delaying an important task at hand—pray. Ask God to help you become a past-procrastinator. Enjoy that bubble bath, but don't procrastinate other tasks. Tell a close friend about your procrastination habits and ask her to be your accountability and prayer partner.

Sometimes you'll need to take baby steps to get a big job accomplished. Small tasks, done over and over, will get the job done. Perhaps when making that to-do list, rather than jot down our tasks in big-job notation, maybe it would be helpful to break it down into smaller steps.

Does the stovetop need to be cleaned? It may sound silly, but jot down these individual tasks. Clean front burners. Clean back burners. Wash knobs. Maybe smaller bullet-points will help you see projects as doable tasks.

Procrastinating rarely solves anything and usually causes stress. That's not God's plan. His plan is to work efficiently in a fitting and orderly way. Lean into him and imagine tackling each little step with him by your side. He is a powerful God of miracles. He can certainly cheer you on through the little steps to complete a big job. He'll support you, encourage you, and carry you through. Just picture him giving you a holy high-five with each accomplishment.

Don't procrastinate, go with God, and watch the stress disappear.

Dear God, please help me to avoid putting off the things that I need to do. My head knows that procrastinating almost always causes me anxious thoughts and unnecessary stress, but I tend to fall into that pattern too easily. Lord, I want to do every job with my whole heart, as if working for you, just as your Word says in Colossians. Whether that's cleaning my stove, tackling a big project at work, or volunteering in my community. When I procrastinate and then rush through the work, I'm not giving you my best. Forgive me for those times, Lord, and help me to stay on task each day. Help me to become a permanent past-procrastinator.

Reflect on the things that push you to procrastinate. What actions do you need to take to minimize those distractions and what strategies can you employ to keep your focus on a task until it's completed?

Over time, chronic procrastination has detrimental effects on a person's mental and physical health and leads to chronic stress, psychological distress, dissatisfaction, depression symptoms, anxiety, poor health decisions, chronic illness, and heart issues.

CHAPTER TWENTY-NINE

Bubbling Over

May the Lord make your love increase and overflow for each other and for everyone else, just as ours does for you.

1 THESSALONIANS 3:12 NIV

Five-year-old Emma eyed the big tub in her mama's bathroom. Mama had said Emma needed a bath. She hadn't mentioned a bubble bath, but Emma didn't think she'd mind. She turned the faucet on and dumped a whole bottle of bubble bath under the stream of water: the gallon-sized economy bottle. Her eyes got big as she saw the tub filling with bubbles. This was going to be awesome. Her mama hadn't ever had this many bubbles before.

Emma realized she'd forgotten to get her clean clothes, so while the water ran and giant bubbles formed in the tub, she walked upstairs to her room. She retrieved her fresh pajamas, but as she walked by her activity table, she realized she hadn't finished coloring the picture to give her daddy when he came home from work.

Then she decided it would be nice to put the colored

picture in an envelope, so she walked downstairs to her daddy's office, and hunted through the drawers and cabinets until she found an envelope. Emma carefully folded the picture, wrote "To Daddy! Love, Emma" on the front, and skipped back down the hall to put his gift in her parents' room.

That's when her little jaw dropped in shock. Bubbles were floating out of the bathroom. Into the bedroom, and across the floor. Bubbles taller than Emma's head filled the bathroom. "Mama!"

Oh my goodness, that little girl had overflowed the tub, filled the bathroom, and soaked Mama and Daddy's bedroom.

Emma's overflow of bathwater and bubbles definitely wasn't planned. But you know what? God wants us to have an overflow in our lives. He wants us to live so close to him that his sweetness wears off on us. And then he wants our love to increase and to overflow into the lives of those who desperately need to know about the love of Jesus. To people who've messed up their lives seemingly beyond repair—but God's love can change them.

Let's overflow into our homes and churches and then send floods of God's love to everyone around us.

Lord, sometimes I'm hesitant to tell others about you. I don't know why, but I keep the message of your love and mercy as if it's a well-kept secret instead of the greatest story ever told. So many people are starving for what I have. For the peace that fills my heart. For the God who soothes my stresses and cares. And for your love that overwhelms me every time I think about it. Father, help my love for you to grow like Emma's giant bubbles and help me to overflow with Jesus to those who need to hear about him, who need God's love to fill those empty places in their hearts and souls.

Why are you sometimes hesitant to tell others about Jesus? Does that make you anxious? Why does God want your love to increase and overflow into the lives of others?

Anxiety levels rise when people feel lonely. When insecure or threatened, cortisol and adrenaline peak in the body which activates the stress response. Feeling loved and connected helps to eliminate anxiety and produces dopamine which causes people to feel better about themselves and about life in general.

CHAPTER THIRTY

He Is Enough

He said to me, "My grace is sufficient for you, for my power is made perfect in weakness." Therefore I will boast all the more gladly about my weaknesses, so that Christ's power may rest on me.

2 CORINTHIANS 12:9 NIV

Hayley pulled up a YouTube video to show her kids a sample of a long-ago talent show. A man ran back and forth in an attempt to keep bowls and plates spinning high in the air on wooden dowels. While the kids laughed at his antics and the poor film quality, Hayley couldn't help but feel a bit of anxiety watching the four-minute video.

As she settled into her bubble bath that night, Hayley thought back to the video and recognized herself in the plate-spinning talent artist. With the responsibilities of homeschooling, volunteering at church, working a part-time job, and trying to be a good wife and mom, Hayley felt exhausted. Add taking care of occasional needs of aging parents, serving on the library board, attending weekly Bible study, and other day-to-day tasks, and Hayley felt like most of her plates were either wobbling or about to fall off and shatter.

Do you feel that way, too? Do you feel like you're running around trying to keep plates (responsibilities) spinning with perfection? The path to perfection is unattainable and defeating. It's not possible. In this world, we will never have perfection.

We can't do it all, and to attempt perfection is maddening and stressful. We often fall short and we sometimes fail. We sin and seek repentance and forgiveness. Then we try again. We can never be enough by the world's standards.

The good news is that we don't have to be enough. It doesn't matter that we're not. What matters is that we know in our hearts that Jesus is enough. He is everything. He is all we need, and he is our hope for every minute of the day. He is sufficient for all of our needs and there's no need to stress.

Our identity and worth do not revolve around the plates we spin. Our identity is found in Christ alone, and the blood he shed on the cross makes us worthy. Stop spinning and relax in that great news.

Dear God, I often feel like I jump out of bed and start running the minute my feet hit the floor. I want to do it all. I feel like I juggle so many plates at one time, and I fear letting one fall. At times, I don't only want to be enough, I want to be more than enough. Yet, all that striving is for naught, because I will never be perfect. God, you are enough and that's all I need to know. Help me to remember that you are all that I will ever need and that you have no trouble carrying all my stresses and anxieties. You are perfection. Help me to place my identity and worth in you alone.

How does juggling too many
responsibilities cause you stress?
Why do you think you might take on
too many responsibilities?

Research has identified the top causes of stress
as job pressure, money, health, relationships, poor
nutrition, media overload, and sleep deprivation.

Chapter Thirty-One

Far More Valuable

"Look at the birds. They don't plant or harvest or store food in barns, for your heavenly Father feeds them. And aren't you far more valuable to him than they are? Can all your worries add a single moment to your life?"

Matthew 6:26-27 nlt

Teresa held back tears as she prepared oatmeal for her children. This was the last of their food. She'd had to add so much water to stretch it that it was more like oatmeal flavored water. Things had been hard for Teresa ever since her husband abandoned her and their seven children. She'd worked two jobs to keep a roof over their heads and put food on the table. They'd managed—barely—until she'd lost the best of the two jobs a few weeks before. The stress was about to do her in.

Teresa's heart ached as she put the bowls of watery oatmeal on the table. She wanted the best for her children, but she was a failure. She didn't even know where their next meal would come from.

She tried to smile as the children climbed on the school bus. Oh, what she'd give for a long bubble bath to soak the stress away, but even slivers of soap were a precious commodity these days. She sat in her tattered recliner and picked up her worn Bible. Jesus was her only answer. "Lord, I don't know how you're going to do it, but my children need food. I'm so anxious and I can't carry this load by myself anymore."

Her ESV Bible opened to Luke 12:24: "Consider the ravens: they neither sow nor reap, they have neither storehouse nor barn, and yet God feeds them. Of how much more value are you than the birds!"

She tried not to stress, but when children are hungry, that's a difficult thing. When school was over, the children ran into the apartment. Her son said, "Mama, what's all the stuff on the porch?"

When Teresa walked outside she discovered God had nudged someone's heart to bring them dozens of boxes of groceries. More than she needed.

Perhaps you're anxious because of deep financial troubles. Sometimes those situations arrive no matter how hard we work, and often there seems to be no way out. Trust Jesus. The God who feeds the ravens knows exactly where you are.

Father, I'm so anxious I don't even feel like I can take a deep breath. I'm in such a mess financially that there doesn't seem to be any way to fix the situation. You don't lie, God, and you have promised to take care of me. I'm going to trust you even though I can't see an answer. Show me what you want me to learn from this situation. Provide the work that I need to pay my bills and to put food on the table. When my finances are in good shape again, make me sensitive to the needs of others around me so I can bless them as you have blessed me.

What burdens do you need to take to God today? When has God provided for you in the past?

If you are worried about money, you're not alone. Money is a common source of stress for American adults. In fact, according to some studies, 72% of adults report feeling stressed about money whether worrying about paying rent or feeling bogged down by debt. This is pretty significant given that financial stress is linked to so many health issues.

CHAPTER THIRTY-TWO

Furry Friends

God looked over all he had made,
and he saw that it was very good!

GENESIS 1:31 NLT

Elsie wasn't prepared to be a widow in her early sixties, but then rarely is anyone prepared for grief and loneliness. The stress of managing the home alone and making ends meet with her salary weighed heavy on her mind. She was glad she had her four-legged, feline friend to keep her company at the end of a long day.

Many of us enjoy the pleasures of having a pet in the home for sheer enjoyment, but research continues to point out the health benefits too. The unconditional love of a furry friend does way more than just keep you company. Pets decrease stress, improve heart health, and offer emotional and social support. Having an animal in the home decreases the stress-hormone, cortisol, and lowers blood pressure. A pet combats loneliness and encourages positive moods.

God thought of everything when he created this world. He knew just what we would need and he threw in extras he knew we would enjoy too. God created animals, specifically domesticated ones, to give us comfort in our loneliness and times of stress. He wanted us to enjoy their company. Isn't it fun when our pets perch on the side of the tub and play with the bubbles from our bath?

God will provide comfort in our distress. He has all the answers. He will be there for us with everything we face. He also knew we might like to hold and pet and snuggle with a furry friend here on earth to soothe some of those feelings tangibly.

If you have a pet, take comfort in knowing that it is a gift from God. If you don't currently own a pet and feel like the stress of the world is getting to you in your loneliness, consider adopting or fostering a pet from a local shelter. If owning a pet is not an option right now, maybe volunteer at the humane society to play with dogs or pet cats. Furry friends make great stress-relievers.

God, there is something about your awesome creations that is calming to my soul. Especially the four-legged ones. Thank you for the gift of pets. You knew I would enjoy them, and you also knew they could comfort me during times of sadness and calm me during times of stress. I thank you, God, for all that you made because your creations truly are good and magnificent. Help me to remember your goodness, each time I snuggle with one of your four-legged gifts, especially when the troubles of this world take my eyes away from you. Thank you for thinking of everything I would need when you created this world.

How can your furry friend soothe your mind at the end of a long day? How can snuggling with your pet remind you of the attributes and character of God?

Pets and therapy animals can help alleviate stress, anxiety, and depression. A recent survey of pet owners revealed that 74% reported mental health improvements directly tied to having a pet.

CHAPTER THIRTY-THREE

At the Beach

He calmed the storm to a whisper and stilled the waves.

PSALM 107:29 NLT

Valerie had been through one storm of life after another. She'd cared for her father for more than a year before God called him home. She'd barely had time to catch her breath from being physically and emotionally exhausted when she had a fall, breaking several bones which required surgery. The recuperation period had been long and pain filled. She and her husband had just sold their home before her fall, and she felt so anxious and guilty that she wasn't able to help with the packing and moving. She had layers upon layers of stress. On more than one day she'd declared, "If I could just have a day at the beach. My toes need to be in the sand."

There's something about a day at the beach that speaks to our souls when times are hard. After the move, Valerie's husband took her to the beach for a few days. God blessed them with perfect weather. The sun warmed her bones and relaxed her while a soft breeze blew by. Colorful beach umbrellas flapped gently in the wind. The ocean stretched out before them in varying hues of blue and green. Valerie's toes enjoyed being there as much as she knew they would. And soon the *whoosh, splash, whoooooosh, splash* of the waves breaking on shore had lulled her into much-needed rest.

She awakened refreshed for the first time in a long time. Who needed a bubble bath when God's giant bathtub was available? Valerie smiled as she listened to children laughing as they played in the water. The antics of scrawny-legged birds scampering down the sand, and seagulls scavenging for food made her chuckle. God even sent dolphins by for her to enjoy as they leapt gracefully in and out of the water.

Sometimes we forget that the God who stills the waves can also still his children. He loves to see them enjoying life—and he knows that when they are stressed and weary, when their shoulders are weighed down with cares, that spending time delighting in what he's made can refresh them for the days ahead.

Dear Lord, I feel as if I've made the rounds from one difficult situation to another these past few months. There wasn't even time to catch my breath before the next stress-filled hardship arrived. Father, you made me. You know your child, and you know I need rest in the middle of what I'm going through. Would you please provide a way for me to spend time somewhere that will provide peace for my soul? You calm the storms in my life. I'm so grateful for that. Thank you for promising rest and thank you for the beautiful places that you've given me to enjoy. Refresh me for the journey ahead.

What places bring peace and rest to your soul when you are anxious? Have you thought to pray and specifically ask God to let you go there?

Science suggests that the rhythm of ocean waves and tides coming in and out can affect the rhythm of the neuronal waves in our brain, encouraging a more peaceful pace of thought. Some scientists refer to the sounds of water as white noise, in which we can hear any number of things and we are able to let go of our thoughts and let the noise wash over us.

CHAPTER THIRTY-FOUR

Be a Blessing

Take advantage of every opportunity to be a blessing to others,
especially to our brothers and sisters in the family of faith!

GALATIANS 6:10 TPT

Melanie was excited about moving to a new
neighborhood. She liked everything about the new house
except the neighbor down the street. He complained about
everything. From the trash can not being put up fast
enough, to the dog being off the leash that one time she
escaped to the car, to being parked on the curb just long
enough for the washing machine delivery. His complaints
unnerved her.

The grouchy neighbor made life miserable for Melanie.
She complained to her friends and she complained to God.
She spent many hours during her bubble baths stewing. She
hated conflict and it always stressed her out. She prayed for
resolution during those long soaks. It gave her such anxiety
just thinking about living like that long-term.

One day, God whispered, "Be kind to him." Melanie

almost laughed out loud and muttered, "You have to be kidding, God." She wasn't thrilled about the idea, but she knew she had to be obedient.

Melanie baked a pound cake, her mother's recipe, and delivered it to his door. He was barely cordial, but his appreciation seemed genuine. On another occasion, Melanie mowed his lawn when she found out he was down with a bad back. She even wrote a get-well note and stuck it in the front door.

She waved when he drove past and collected his newspapers from the sidewalk and put them on the front porch when he was out of town. And she prayed. For her heart, for his heart, and for God to lead her to be kind to others.

Six months later, the unbelievable happened. The grouchy neighbor dropped by with cookies and an apology.

Prayer and kindness changes people. Hearts are softened—those of the givers and the receivers. God doesn't ask us to be kind to only those who are kind to us. He wants us to be kind to all. In fact, he commands it. He sent his Son for the whole world, and that's always reason enough for kindness.

Dear God, help me be kind to others. Every person belongs to you and is your child. Help me to look for ways to be a blessing to others. You command kindness. Sometimes that's not easy, God, especially when I have a conflict with another person who causes me such anxiety and stress. You don't put qualifications in your Word on who I should be nice to. You never say, "Be nice to the nice ones." Father, your Word is clear. Ephesians 4:32 instructs me to be kind to others and to be tenderhearted toward them, forgiving them as you've forgiven me. Help me to be all of those things. Oh, and thank you, God, for loving me and treating me with such kindness.

How does unresolved conflict take your
focus off Jesus and cause you stress? Is there
someone you need to settle a conflict with?

A recent study of 650 adults found that prolonged
or repetitive conflict resulted in a higher number
of health issues that included such conditions
like chronic headaches, colds, the flu, and back
or neck pain. Researchers determined that stress
from ongoing conflict weakened the participants'
immune systems.

Chapter Thirty-Five

Gathered Together

"Again, truly I tell you that if two of you on earth agree about anything they ask for, it will be done for them by my Father in heaven. For where two or three gather in my name, there am I with them."

MATTHEW 18:19-20 NIV

Opal and Sandra are co-authors. They live in different parts of the country, so most of their work is done through email. The two had a tight book deadline. They had worked on numerous projects together before, but for some reason, despite them praying for each other, this book had been so stressful to write. Like off the charts stressful.

Opal was relieved when Sandra mentioned she was having a hard time with it. Opal thought she'd been the only one struggling. "No," Sandra replied. "Yesterday was so difficult that I felt like I was bleeding on the keyboard. I told my friend I should have chosen an easier job like gold mining."

They kept working, but both were stressed because it felt as if each chapter were being laboriously pulled from them instead of flowing freely. They were taking three times longer to write than usual. Both women were exhausted, and bubble baths weren't helping at all to relax them.

One day it clicked for Sandra. There was a reason why they were having so much trouble. It was because their book would help women draw closer to God, and the devil is always opposed to that idea.

Sandra remembered the Scripture about two or three gathering together and asking their Father for what they needed. She called Opal and said, "This is spiritual. We're going to pray together and ask God to get Satan off our backs while we're writing."

The two women had a sweet time praying together. While they prayed, the stress and anxiety that had been weighing so heavily on them disappeared. They accomplished more work that afternoon than they had done in several days.

Are you weighed down and stressed today? There's something powerful about praying together with someone. As Opal and Sandra learned, their party of two was really a party of three, because as he had promised, God was there with them. He will be with you as well.

Father, I want to serve you and want you to be pleased with me. There are tasks you've placed on my heart, yet I feel like I've been in a battle the whole way through. It's stressful, exhausting, and frustrating. When days of spiritual warfare arrive, remind me that I don't have to go through difficult places of life by myself. Give me faith-filled friends who will pray with me. Thank you for the assurance that you are with me. Remind me that all power lies in you and that my strength and ability to fulfill your plans for me will only happen through your strength.

Can you remember a time when you were going through spiritual warfare? How can praying together with a friend make a difference during those times?

God reminds us in his Word to stay aware of Satan's schemes, to live alert in this world, and to stay close to him. He equips us with strength, wisdom, and discernment through his Spirit to stay strong in the spiritual warfare battle. He invites us to spend time in his presence, through prayer and worship, pressing in to know him more.

CHAPTER THIRTY-SIX

Do Accordingly

"Since I, your Lord and Teacher, have washed your feet,
you ought to wash each other's feet."

JOHN 13:14 NLT

Do you ever stop to think about the challenges Jesus faced during his journeys with the disciples? Walking long distances on dusty, rocky roads in sandal-clad feet. The unwelcoming meanness of naysayers. The unending lists of requests. The taunts and jeers of those in authority. It's just about more stress than one could bear.

Yet, through it all, Jesus wanted to serve. His compassion for others is unsurpassed. He met the needs—physical and emotional—of those who flocked to his side. And he knew his greatest gift of service to mankind was death on the cross, to save us from a life in hell and bring us to eternity in heaven with him. While he walked this earth, he served.

Can you imagine what it might have felt like to have the Savior of the world wash your feet? Jesus chose one of the dirtiest parts of the body to wash. He wrapped a towel around his waist, pushed up his sleeves, and got dirty for the sake of his followers. He took on the job of the lowly servant and willingly cleaned the disciples' feet.

Sometimes the best stress relief at the end of the day comes in the form of serving another person. Jesus explained to his disciples that no servant was greater than his master and no messenger greater than the one who sent him. He said, "Now that you know these things, God will bless you for doing them."

At the end of a long day, if you find yourself thinking, *If anybody else makes one more request or has one more need, I'm gonna lose it*, perhaps humbly serving is just the stressbuster you need.

Rather than become exasperated with one more task, let's love and serve genuinely like Jesus did. Run the water for a relaxing bath for someone in your house. Fill the tub with bubbles. Offer a foot massage. Serve like Jesus and wash your stress away.

Dear God, thank you for my family. When I get exasperated at the end of the day because somebody needs one more thing, remind me of the story of Jesus washing his disciples' feet. I know that you command me to serve those outside of my family; stir in me a desire to humbly serve those I love most—those under the same roof as me. Help me not to allow the stress of a long day to cause me to be short-tempered with those I love. Refresh and renew me so I can give my very best to those closest to me instead of my leftovers from a long day.

Why is it so easy to take out the frustrations of a long day on the ones you love the most? What are three tangible ways to express your love to family members each day?

In Bible times, when guests came to an ordinary home, clad in sandals and dusty, dirty feet, the host provided the water and the guests washed their own feet. However, in wealthier homes, slaves washed sojourners' feet. It was considered a lowly job, fit only for a servant or slave.

CHAPTER THIRTY-SEVEN

The Guest List

*Whenever my busy thoughts were out of control,
the soothing comfort of your presence
calmed me down and overwhelmed me with delight.*

PSALM 94:19 TPT

Amanda had been so excited about getting married until the planning began. Everybody had ideas of what she and Brandon should have at their wedding. Nobody was shy about voicing their opinions. She'd never felt such stress before.

Amanda wanted a simple wedding cake, but when they met with the baker, everyone in the family pulled out pictures of fancy wedding cakes and made suggestions for decorations they thought should be added. A similar situation occurred when they visited the florist. Amanda's stress ratcheted up a notch.

Her dad didn't mean to be a downer, but she'd overheard him telling her mom he didn't know how they were going to pay for everything, that things were becoming too extravagant.

It was all too much. Amanda escaped to a bubble bath. As she sat there soaking, she uttered a desperate prayer, "God, my mind is whirling and everything is out of control. Will you help me?"

She couldn't explain it, but over the next few hours, God sent her a sweet unexplainable calmness. And he gave her an answer. Amanda called Brandon. The two talked and then set up a joint family meeting.

Amanda said, "We appreciate your excitement for planning the wedding, but here's what we want. We don't want a fancy wedding that will cost a fortune. Mama, your wedding gown was gorgeous and I've always wanted to wear it for my wedding. Can I do that?"

Brandon said, "Mom, could we have the reception in our backyard? Your garden is beautiful. I've always wanted my reception there." Both moms were wiping tears as they nodded yes.

Brandon and Amanda held hands as they said, "The most important thing for both of us is to have God at the center of our wedding and our marriage. As long as that happens, we'll be thrilled."

An hour later, the wedding was planned, sweet memories were made, and God was honored. Later that night, bride-to-be Amanda went to bed calmed by God and overwhelmed with delight.

Father, I want you to be the center of my life. I don't want to be filled with stress or irritable as a result of big events. I want to look back on the days of planning as happy and productive. Thank you for answering my prayers, for calming all the busy thoughts that race through my mind and make me anxious. Feeling your presence has made all the difference. God, I invite you to be the special guest in my life. You have overwhelmed me with delight.

Why are big events so stressful? What difference does it make to ask God to be the special guest? How can that relieve your stress and anxiety?

Some clear signs that you might be dealing with event-related stress include feeling tired, drained, and exhausted. You may be worried and anxious when you think about anything event related, procrastinating on your plans due to feeling overwhelmed. You might even feel like you have a huge weight sitting on your shoulders that just won't go away.

CHAPTER THIRTY-EIGHT

Watch and See

The LORD will fight for you;
you need only to be still.

EXODUS 14:14 NIV

Just when the Israelites thought they could catch their breath, Pharaoh reneged on his promise to let God's enslaved people go. He gathered the troops for a mighty pursuit. The Israelites were terrified. Ahead lay the impassable Red Sea and behind lay the formidable Egyptian army. Talk about stress.

But God.

The Israelites' predicament hadn't caught God off-guard. In fact, he had magnificent plans to reveal his glory to the Israelites, to the Egyptians, and ultimately, to the world.

Obeying God's instructions, Moses stretched out his hand over the sea. God pushed back millions of gallons of water, leaving a path of dry ground. On either side of the path, a monstrous wall of water stood menacingly.

Astounded, the Israelites stepped out in faith and walked on dry ground to the other side. When the last one of God's chosen people stepped safely on the other side, Moses, again in obedience to God, stretched out his hand over the sea and the mighty waters fell crashing and gurgling back into place, wiping out the Egyptian army.

The water that threatened to destroy the Israelites in the beginning served as a wall of protection and then a means to defeat evil. It was a miracle that only the Almighty God in heaven could perform. God's glorious power over the waters of the Red Sea served as a visible sign of his protection over his chosen people and the execution of judgment over evil.

When we feel like we're surrounded by enemies on all sides, when we struggle to overcome difficulties surrounding us, when we feel like this world is going to take us down, we need not worry, for our heavenly Father will fight for us. The battle is his. God's power is just as mighty today as it was in Moses' day. God still performs miracles.

The Israelites stepped onto the dry land in faith and obedience. Despite our worries and anxieties, let's step out in faith and obedience even when trouble surrounds. Then let's watch and see what God will do.

Oh, God, sometimes I am so anxious with troubles ahead and challenges behind, with difficulties to my right and left. I'm often paralyzed with fear and afraid to move forward. God, you have promised that you will fight for me, you will go before me and behind me. You have told me in your Word that whether I turn to the right or to the left you are there. You never, ever leave me. You will take care of me. You fight for me and you stand for righteousness. You will not let me drown. How could I possibly be stressed when you are in control? Your power is unfathomable. I am forever grateful for your presence.

How does God's provision and protection from yesterday give you hope for tomorrow? What assurance do you have that God is with you always? How does that impact your anxiety over situations?

Imagine being a servant-leader just to free the Israelites from Egyptian slavery. Remember that faith is not about having lesser levels of stress or achieving success in life but on how we put our trust and belief in God in the middle of these situations.

CHAPTER THIRTY-NINE

Clean House

All things should be done decently and in order.

1 CORINTHIANS 14:40 ESV

Allison looked at her messy house. She wanted to climb back into her unmade bed and pull the covers over her head. Every room was so cluttered it was depressing. It stressed her out just looking at it. How had she let it get like that? She was so overwhelmed that she didn't have a clue where to start. She'd go take a bubble bath instead, but that would require cleaning the tub, removing the toys, and climbing over the wet towels on the floor.

She'd once kept a spotless home, but then some things happened that had caused her to become depressed. She'd quit caring. Now her messy house was causing her more depression and stress.

Allison prayed, "God, this is bigger than me. Actually, it might be bigger than five people. Will you show me how to get my house and life in order? Make me ruthless when it comes to getting rid of things I don't need to keep."

She put trash in one large bag and give-away items in the other. The things she planned to keep would be put up where they belonged if she could remember where that was.

It took several months before her house was clean and the clutter was gone, but, oh how it made her feel better. The stress had disappeared and the uncluttered rooms made her heart happy.

It often isn't just our homes that need work. Sometimes we quit paying attention and then discover that our spiritual lives are just as messy and cluttered as our homes are. The only way to fix the problem is to take that first step and get started. To pray and say, "God, this is bigger than me. I'm going to need some help. Make me ruthless when it comes to getting rid of things in my life I don't need to keep."

Consistent effort is required to keep a clean heart. We must throw the junk away. We must work until our souls sparkle and shine for Jesus. Having things in order spiritually will definitely make our hearts happy.

Father, it must have been so disappointing for you to look at the condition of my heart and see the sloppy mess it had become. Remove the stresses of life that keep me from paying attention to my soul. Just as Allison was ruthless when it came to getting rid of the clutter in her home, make me ruthless when it comes to getting rid of the sin in my heart. Help me to spend time in prayer and in your Word. Put a spotlight on the places I need to focus my attention. Help my soul to sparkle and shine for you. Keep my heart pure and clean. I want to please you, and I want to have my spiritual house in order.

How can a messy house cause stress and anxiety? How can a messy spiritual life affect you and others?

Clutter can play a significant role in our level of stress. How we feel about our homes, our workplaces, and ourselves is important. Messy homes and workspaces can leave us feeling anxious, helpless, and overwhelmed.

Chapter Forty

Up and at 'Em

Since we are surrounded by such a great cloud of witnesses,
let us throw off everything that hinders and the sin that
so easily entangles. And let us run with perseverance the race
marked out for us.

Hebrews 12:1 NIV

One of the last things we might think of doing after a long, stressful day is an activity that makes us break out in a sweat. It's a proven fact, however, that physical activity can enhance those feel-good endorphins and other chemicals in the brain and body, leading to a better mood and removing the stress of the day's irritations. Some cardiologists recommend a minimum of at least twenty minutes of exercise three times a week for heart health, but more is even better.

Even with a busy schedule, we should fit in time for physical activity. Not only will it serve as a stress-reliever, we'll feel better and stay healthier. Consider walking, jogging, biking, swimming, jumping on a trampoline, or playing group sports. How about gardening, housecleaning, raking leaves, or even mowing the lawn for exercise?

When possible, let's include others. We can bond, get healthy, and de-stress together. It's a great time to catch up, to laugh together, or to make plans for other hang out times. It's a wonderful time to look for examples that remind us of Jesus too.

Combine prayer time with the night's physical activity. We can ask God to remove the day's frustrations and supply peace. After we unwind with exercise and prayer, then it's time to sink into a warm bubble bath to wash away any remaining stressful thoughts.

Erase the cares of the day in that bubble bath. Remove every anxious thought and focus completely on God. Think of his goodness and faithfulness. Thank him for his provisions and blessings. Praise him for salvation and grace and mercy. Thank him for his life and his death. Thank him for how good he is. Focus on God for the entire bubble bath without letting any external thought crowd your mind.

Then when you're wrinkly as a prune, pull the stopper and watch the cares drain away.

Dear God, sometimes the last thing I want to do after a long day is exercise. Give me a little nudge when I hesitate to take care of my own health. Lord, I know the importance of a healthy body to help me manage stress. Help me to find the time to do what I need to do to stay healthy and active because I know that my body needs it. Help me to eat healthy, to exercise, and avoid those things that are not good. Help me to treat my body as your temple just like you say in your Word. Thank you, God, for caring about my health. Help me to show the same concern.

How can a healthy body help you focus
more on God? How can feeling your
best physically help you have
less anxious thoughts?

Regular aerobic exercise will bring remarkable
changes to your body, your metabolism, your
heart, and your spirits. It has a unique capacity to
exhilarate and relax, to provide stimulation and
calm, to counter depression and dissipate stress.

CHAPTER FORTY-ONE

Stress Be Gone

Don't be pulled in different directions or worried about a thing.
Be saturated in prayer throughout each day, offering your
faith-filled requests before God with overflowing gratitude. Tell
him every detail of your life, then God's wonderful peace that
transcends human understanding, will make the answers known
to you through Jesus Christ.

PHILIPPIANS 4:6–7 TPT

We all know that stress and anxiety aren't good for us,
but how are we supposed to get rid of them? Angela had
been going through an especially stressful time. She needed
relief so she posted on Facebook and asked her friends to tell
what things stressed them and also to share what they did
to relieve stress. Angela was fascinated by the results. First,
she was floored by the number of people who responded. It
seemed she wasn't the only one plagued by anxiety. Second,
she discovered they had a wide variety of ways that they
dealt with stress.

Some mentioned they lowered the stress levels by talking

with friends, planning an impromptu lunch date, spending time with sisters in Christ, having game night or watching a movie with their families, or... taking a bubble bath.

Others said that baking, painting, or doing something new with their home decor relaxed them. There's something about being creative that takes our minds off our troubles.

Playing music and singing also topped the lists. That's interesting because in the Bible, there are numerous instances of the Israelites singing while God fought their battles and gave them victory.

Exercise was one of the ways many of Angela's friends said they de-stressed. Riding bikes and walking on the beach or in the country were favorites because they could also enjoy God's creation. Several people said that watching and listening to online videos of the outdoors could even be relaxing.

Reading a book by one of your favorite authors is another great way to remove you from your stressors. Reading clears your mind and transports you to places far away from your problems.

The key is finding what works for you.

Of course, the best way is going to Jesus with our problems, spending time in his Word, and praying. He loves us and his heart is touched by what touches us. He's the one who can fix the situations, reconcile the relationships, and calm his child in the chaos. And he's willing to carry our burdens for us. Nothing relieves stress like that.

Father, you made me and you know my heart. You knew there would be many times in my life when I'd be stressed by my circumstances. Yes, even moments where I'd feel like I was going to explode from the pressure. Thank you for giving me so many ways to de-stress, to relieve the anxieties of life. Help me to trust you more with the issues I face, to turn my problems over to you and leave them with you instead of picking them back up again. Thank you for fighting my battles for me and for the victories you give me. I couldn't make it through a day without you and I'm so grateful I never have to worry about that.

What causes you the most stress?
What are the best ways
for you to de-stress?

While classical music has a particularly soothing effect—it slows heart rate, lowers blood pressure, and decreases levels of stress hormones—any music that you love will flood your brain with feel-good neurochemicals like dopamine, and that can combat stress.

CHAPTER FORTY-TWO

God's Perfect Peace

May the Lord himself, the Lord of peace, pour into you
his peace in every circumstance and in every possible way.
The Lord's tangible presence be with you all.

2 THESSALONIANS 3:16 TPT

A tidal pool, a shallow, isolated pocket of seawater found
in areas where the ocean meets the land, is home to many
of God's beautiful sea creatures. Miniscule in comparison to
the creations that swim in ocean bathwaters, creatures like
anemones, sea stars, snails, barnacles, mussels, seaweed, and
small crabs face huge challenges with the ebb and flow of
the tides.

It might be like a community hot tub for sea creatures,
but it comes with its share of stress. Animals in a tide pool
face the challenges of crashing waves in high tide and
diminished moisture during low tide. Temperatures and salt
content change frequently, and open waters make the tiny
animals vulnerable to predators.

God provided for these tiny beauties. Some camouflage

themselves from predators by attaching to rocks or plants with their spines. Others blend in with their surroundings, and some bury into the sand below. Shells and exoskeletons keep predators away and bodies moist. Tube feet help sea urchins and sea stars cling to rocks or seaweed. Barnacles cling to one another for protection.

God makes a way for us when we're stressed, too. If God can provide stress-relief adaptations for those beautiful, yet tiny, little sea creatures, then he can certainly help us deal with stress too.

God gives us families and friends who love and support us. He gives us a community of believers to cling to in our time of need. He equips us with the brains and intelligence to make adaptations and changes to help us deal with stress. He provides us with spiritual mentors, godly counselors, and medical professionals to help us sort through our challenges.

Most of all, God gave us Jesus, the Rock, to cling to in our time of stress. When we cling to him, no crashing wave can tumble us. No predator can snatch us. The elements around us will not destroy us. God loves us and he cares for us deeply.

Dear God, thank you for that perfect peace that comes from you and you alone. I can't do this on my own, God. I need you. Help me to cling to you. You are my rock. I need you for big problems, for little annoyances, and for everything in-between. Father, this life is too difficult without you. I'm grateful that you are the Almighty God who can handle all of my huge difficulties. Thank you that you care about and take care of my seemingly little problems too. God, help me to turn all of my cares over to you and live in your peace. I don't want the world's problems to bring me down. Let me give them to you and live with joy.

How does focusing on God's peace in all circumstances help you face individual challenges? Write down some challenges that you've faced in the past. Beside each one, write how God provided for you during that circumstance.

Christians aren't immune to stress. Here are a few healthy ways to deal with stress: recognize the problem, give yourself a break, get help, pray, meditate on the Word of God, and spend time giving thanks.

CHAPTER FORTY-THREE

Mountains of Papers

Here's what I've learned through it all:
Leave all your cares and anxieties at the feet of the Lord,
and measureless grace will strengthen you.

PSALM 55:22 TPT

Dianne shook her head as she looked at the mountains of papers on her dining room table. With a business that operated in multiple states and counties, the weeks leading up to April 15 were one of the most stressful times of the year for her. Yes, the dreaded tax season. Unfortunately for Dianne, her business was still small, so she couldn't afford staff to do the paperwork for her throughout the year. She'd meant to work on it a little each month, but life had been so busy she hadn't had time. Hence, the mountains of papers and a gargantuan task ahead of her.

There's an old saying, "There are two certain things in life: death and taxes." Both felt about the same now to Dianne. The IRS would probably never deal with a more honest woman, but she was always anxious she'd miss something and a dreaded audit would come her way. She was meticulous as she worked on the paperwork, and she knew that many days of boring stressful work was ahead of her.

Underlying all of that was the stress of wondering how much she'd owe this year. It seemed no matter how much she paid in, she always owed more. What she really wanted to do was to throw the papers in a huge box, put everything out of her mind, and go take a long bubble bath. But she knew that wasn't an option.

Are you stressed by tax time, mountains of papers, or dealing with government entities and all the red tape that's involved? Those anxiety-causing scenarios are even more stressful because we aren't in control of any of it. Somebody else is.

That's a wonderful reminder that when we end up in situations like those, we have someone we can go to who is in control. He'll be with us while we tame the mountains of papers. He'll help us when we've talked to the 27th person as we try to work our way through red tape. We can count on him to *always* be with us—even through death and taxes.

Lord, I'm overwhelmed by the size of the task in front of me. There's so much to do and so little time to do it. You're the God who calms the storms. Will you please calm your child today? I'm so stressed by this. I feel completely out of control which makes me extra grateful that I have the assurance that you are always in control of me and anything that affects my life. Today, Lord, I place it all in your hands knowing that's the best place it can be. Instead of being grouchy about having to do my taxes, let them be a reminder of how you've given me income and sweet blessings along the way.

Why is tax season (or dealing with government agencies) sometimes so stressful? What steps can you take to make that process less stressful?

Tax season can be very stressful. Days are filled with time-consuming tasks like compiling financial information and trudging through various tax forms. Perhaps more than ever, it's important to relax, especially considering that stress can contribute to heart disease, obesity, diabetes, and high blood pressure.

CHAPTER FORTY-FOUR

Laugh Out Loud

When the cares of my heart are many,
your consolations cheer my soul.

PSALM 94:19 ESV

Have you ever been in the middle of a stressful time and then something made you laugh until your stomach hurt? Isn't it amazing how the cares of life float away when that happens? It's especially awesome to hear someone whose laughter is so contagious that everyone is soon laughing with them.

When was the last time you had an all-out belly laugh? Most of us don't have enough of those. Do you snort when you laugh or is your laughter dainty and giggle-like? Types of laughter vary so much that there are more than a dozen words to describe different forms of laughter. No matter how you laugh, it's always good for whatever ails you.

While laughter won't alleviate the causes of stress in your life, it can help you feel better, which in turn leads to relaxation and the renewed ability to face what's going on.

Mental health professionals have researched and compiled quite a list of the healthy benefits of laughter.

The physical act of laughing triggers the release of endorphins, those feel-good chemicals the body produces. Laughter decreases stress hormones like cortisol and increases infection-fighting antibodies. Laughing helps you stay healthy. It increases blood flow which helps prevent heart disease. Prescribe a daily dose of laughter for better well-being.

In Ecclesiastes 3:4, it says that there's a time to weep and a time to laugh. God made laughter and he wants us to enjoy it. There's not a better glue to bond people together than shared laughter. Those are the priceless moments where sweet memories are made.

God wants us to be full of laughter and to share that joy with others. The next time you settle into a warm bubble bath, remember the funny things that happened during the day, and laugh out loud as you soak the stress away.

Dear God, help me to remember that you are the creator of laughter. Laughter has so often eased my stress and worries. I thank you for such a special gift, and I'm so grateful that you created our bodies in such a way that laughter physically improves my health and well-being as well as just simply being fun. Help me to find friends to laugh with, things to laugh about, and something to smile about every day, no matter how stressful my life has been. Help me to keep in mind how valuable laughter is to my body and help me to find ways to make others around me enjoy some laughter too.

How has God used laughter to help you get through stressful times? Why do you think God tied laughter and improved health together?

A good, vigorous laugh produces enough endorphins to relieve pain, physical tension, and stress, leaving your muscles relaxed for almost an hour afterward.

CHAPTER FORTY-FIVE

Sweet Like Taffy

When my spirit faints within me,
you know my way!

PSALM 142:3 ESV

Have you ever been to a candy store and watched them make their sweet treats? There's a candy place that has large windows around its store. Folks watch with interest as caramel apples are dipped and fudge is made. There are also days when they make taffy.

A sugar syrup is cooked and then flavors and colors are added. At this point, it's poured onto a huge oiled marble slab. The candy-maker flips and folds it with a spatula until it's cool enough to handle. But care must still be taken, because while it often seems cool on the outside it can still be hot on the inside.

The candy is rolled into a rope-like shape and then pulled and twisted—again and again and again until the taffy becomes glossy. After several more steps, it's rolled into a rope shape, cut into pieces, and wrapped in paper.

You might not realize it, but we are taffy. Not literally of course. Haven't you had days where it's felt as if you've been pulled in a dozen different directions? Think about it. You start your bubble bath water and then you hear, "I need help.", or the dryer beeps, the dog barks to go outside, or the phone rings. Yes, we're pulled in a dozen different directions. It's stressful, especially when we were already exhausted before all the pulling began. Like the taffy, we may appear cool on the outside, but we're sometimes hot on the inside.

Our spirits are faint within us, and we need to get rid of the stress. When we're in the midst of these times, God says he knows our way. He can strengthen us, refresh us, and give us joy as we're pulled from task to task.

Father, there are days when I feel as if I'm at the end of my rope. There's nothing left, physically, spiritually, or emotionally. Yet my responsibilities and my family keep pulling on me to help with their various needs. I'll be honest. Sometimes I feel as if I'm simmering under the surface. My spirit is overwhelmed and I am less than sweet as I care for my family. Stress rules me at those times. I'm so grateful that you know my way. That none of these things come as a surprise to you. Strengthen me, Lord. I want to be a kind and loving woman, mom, and wife. Help the sweetness of Jesus to wear off on me.

How does stress affect you when you feel like you're being pulled in a dozen different directions? How can hanging out with Jesus make you sweet like taffy?

Feeling overwhelmed and stressed from being too busy has become a way of life for many people. Life does not have to be this way. You can have a balanced life and handle the demands you face each day. You can be in control. The most critical ingredient is you. It is up to you to take responsibility for your own wellbeing and lighten the load where necessary.

CHAPTER FORTY-SIX

Loving Arms

Pour our all your worries and stress upon him and leave them there,
for he always tenderly cares for you.

1 PETER 5:7 TPT

Grandma Peg usually liked giving Ben a bath. Lathering up his dark hair and wiping his face. Washing those soft, dimpled hands and feet. Bathing the tiny little fingers and pudgy toes. Pouring suds over wrinkled baby belly and back. Then watching while her grandson splashed and kicked and delighted in the warm water. Not this time though. He was overtired from a busy day and wanted nothing to do with bath time.

The crying began when she started the water in the tub and began to strip off his shirt. She bathed him as quickly as possible, while tears dripped off his cheeks into the water. When she wrapped him in the fluffy towel, his lavender-scented body relaxed in her arms and he stopped crying immediately. Clad in footie pajamas, Ben snuggled deep into Grandma Peg's arms, his eyes getting heavy and his breathing growing deep.

Do you ever wish you could snuggle deep into your heavenly Father's arms? Especially when you're overtired from all the struggles of the day? When you just want to lean back and tell him all of your problems and cares and worries. And you just want to be held. Like a child again. With soothing promises that everything is going to be okay.

This is available to us at any time. God bids us to come to him, to pour out all our worries and stress upon him and to leave it with him because he cares so tenderly for us. Just as tenderly as we've cared for a little one fresh out of the tub.

God wants to hold us in his care. To wrap his arms around us in love. To listen to the stresses and cares of the day. To wash away all of our worries and fears. To comfort us and give us hope, and to say to us, "Everything's going to be okay."

When you've had a rough day, step out of the bubble bath and into a warm bathrobe. Then sit quietly and imagine yourself wrapped in God's loving arms. He cares for you.

Dear God, when I'm overtired from the stress of the day, help me to remember how tenderly you care for me. Help me to give you all my worries and not to take them back five minutes later. Let me rest in the comfort of knowing that you'll take care of all those things that cause me stress. Help me to feel your loving arms around me, holding me tenderly. Help my stress to melt away, to drain from my weary body, and help me to relax in the comfort of your arms. When life gets busy and stressful again, help me to feel your presence right there next to me. Help me to remember your faithfulness and keep me close to you always.

How might your struggles and challenges draw you closer to God? Is there someone you know who's traveling a difficult journey? How can you come alongside them and be an encouragement?

The use of lavender scents has proven to be beneficial to sleep, which is why many baby soaps and shampoos are lavender scented. The aroma of lavender can slow down heart rate and blood pressure and put the body in a relaxed and calm state.

Through God's Eyes

Do all that you can to live in peace with everyone.

ROMANS 12:18 NLT

Marie had hoped to be friends with her mother-in-law when she got married, but that's not the way things happened. When Jared introduced Marie to his mom, Patricia, Marie was met with coolness.

Things hadn't improved throughout the months of Marie and Jared's engagement. When Marie tried to hug Patricia at the wedding reception and called her "Mom," Patricia said, "I'm *Jared's* mother. You may call me Patricia."

The situation made Marie anxious, but she didn't know what to do. Things went downhill even more after the young couple returned from their honeymoon and Patricia showed up at their house with cleaning supplies. She said, "I've come to show you the right way to clean."

When Marie asked Patricia if she'd share her recipe for Jared's favorite mint brownies, Patricia replied, "I'll be the one to make those for my son." Marie was crushed. She didn't say anything to Jared but she cried heartbroken tears while in her bubble bath. The holidays were coming soon. Being around Patricia was so stressful. How would Marie survive the family get-togethers?

One night, Jared shared how his mom grew up in an orphanage. She'd been abused as a child, growing up without love or even basic kindness. Then Marie heard God whisper to her soul, "Pray about your relationship with her."

That night before Marie went to sleep, she prayed, "Lord, help me to see Patricia as you see her. Please reduce the stress of being around her and help me to love her."

The situation didn't change overnight, but Marie's heart did. One evening soon thereafter, Marie went up to Patricia after dinner and sincerely said, "Patricia, I love you. Thank you for raising such a wonderful son."

What Marie didn't realize was that other than her husband and son, nobody had ever said the words "I love you" to Patricia. They had a long journey ahead, but healing in their relationship began that night.

When we see others as Jesus does, and we respond with his love, our stress disappears and things change.

Father, it's hard being around unpleasant people especially when they've hurt me. Conflict stresses me out, especially when it's in my family. I don't know how to fix things, and to be honest, sometimes I don't even want to. I know that's not pleasing to you. I realize that wounded people wound others. Help me to see those who've hurt me through your eyes. Help me to love them like you do even when it's not warranted. Give me your mercy and grace for them. Take my anxious thoughts and replace them with your peace. Thank you for loving me even when I don't deserve it and help me to do the same for those who hurt me.

Why do you think in-law relationships
can sometimes be so stressful? How does
it make a difference when you try to see
others through God's eyes?

In-law troubles are not uncommon. Approximately
75% of married couples experience frequent and
extreme in-law conflicts.

CHAPTER FORTY-EIGHT

Complete Trust

Trust in the LORD with all your heart;
do not depend on your own understanding.

PROVERBS 3:5 NLT

Never leave a baby unattended in a bathtub. What parent doesn't know that rule? Can you just imagine the anxiety Jochebed must have felt about placing her three-month-old baby in a basket and leaving him at the edge of the Nile River? Would he drown? Would the crocodiles snatch him?

Moses' mother hid him as long as she could. For three months, Jochebed cradled her precious son in her arms, tucked away in hopes that the Egyptian soldiers wouldn't find and kill him. Pharaoh had ordered the killing of every Hebrew boy because their numbers were increasing rapidly and Pharaoh feared a rebellion.

Can you imagine living with that kind of stress? Every time Jochebed heard voices outside her window or footsteps near the door, she panicked. Every time her hungry newborn cried out during the middle of the night, she jumped.

When she could hide him no more, Jochebed kissed her sweet baby on the cheek and breathed in his smell one last time. She swaddled him in cloths and tucked him inside a handmade basket.

Then, she set the basket afloat among the reeds along the bank of the Nile River. With instructions to her daughter to watch from a short distance away, Jochebed turned and walked home. Surely her vision was obscured with tears.

Jochebed may or may not have known that Pharaoh's daughter would come to that very spot to bathe. When Miriam offered to get a Hebrew woman to nurse the baby, Moses was returned to his mom's care until that time when he went to live in Pharaoh's palace. Jochebed couldn't have known how God would solve her dilemma, but she trusted him when she placed baby Moses in the Nile River.

That needs to be us. We can trust God with our stresses and anxieties. He has proven himself faithful. We can count on him even when we don't understand. Our hearts may ache and we might be at a loss for answers, but just as he took care of baby Moses, God will care for us as well.

God, I'll admit that it's hard to trust completely when the stakes are high. When my marriage hits a snag. When I lose a big promotion to someone else. When something happens to one of my kids. When a friend disappoints me. When credit collectors are banging on my door. But God, my trust shouldn't be dependent on the situation. Your Word says to trust in you. It's a command. When I'm stressed or burdened with a mountain of cares, please help me to obey. I can never understand the whole picture, and that's why I need to trust and leave the rest to you. You are the Almighty God who will not let me down. I will trust in you with full confidence.

In what circumstances do you tend to have the most trouble trusting God? What steps can you take to change that?

Though firm numbers are unavailable, estimates state that up to two hundred people die each year in the jaws of a Nile crocodile. Perhaps that makes the story of Jochebed trusting God with her son even more amazing.

CHAPTER FORTY-NINE

Facing the Unknown

The LORD himself goes before you and will be with you;
he will never leave you nor forsake you.
Do not be afraid; do not be discouraged.

DEUTERONOMY 31:8 NIV

Have you ever had a fear of the unknown, stressing about the uncertainty of things that lie ahead? Most of us have probably done that, and it's amazing what big imaginations we have in the middle of those moments.

I suspect Sarai had those anxieties when Abraham told her they were going on a journey to the land where God had called him, but he had no idea of exactly where that would be. Most wives would have been perturbed about that. Can you imagine if a husband came home and told his wife they were moving but he didn't know where?

Can you picture the stress and uncertainty that Mrs. Noah must have felt when Noah came home and told her what God had told him to do?

Those moments didn't just happen during Bible times.

Teresa had those anxieties when the doctor told her she had cancer. She'd never been down that path before, and the unknown was scary. Even the medical tests were stressful because she'd never had an MRI or cat scan and she didn't know what to expect. She was stressed about going through chemo treatments. She was stressed about losing her hair. And she was stressed about whether she'd live or die. She didn't want her husband to know how anxious she was, but her bubble bath moments were filled with tears and desperate prayers.

Darlene was excited about the new baby that would soon join their family. It was their first, and she didn't tell anyone, but she was stressed about childbirth and about being a mother because all of that was unknown to her.

Here's the marvelous thing about all those unknown moments. God isn't surprised by any of them, and he's never faced an unknown situation. He's already been everywhere that we'll be going. He will be with us every step of the way. When we get there, we'll discover that he has already equipped us with everything we need to make it through.

Lord, it seems I worry too much and trust too little. When I'm faced with new situations where I've never been before, it fills me with anxiety. I don't know why, but I always seem to imagine the worst. I stress over all the things that might happen. Help me to place the unknown in your hands. Thank you for the assurance that you've already been wherever you've asked me to go. I'm grateful that with the beauty of hindsight, I can look back at past situations and see that you equipped me with the strength, courage, and grace to get through the unknown. Instead of stressing, help me to trust. Remind me that you're a faithful God.

Why do you think the unknown is so stressful? How does it change your stress level to know that God has never faced an unknown situation?

Anxiety is fear of the unknown. An impending sense of uncertainty, or a stress response to a perceived threat in the future. The brain and body are often caught up in sensations and feelings of tension, or a sense of apprehension, that keeps the mind locked into a cycle of excessive worry, anticipation, and panic.

CHAPTER FIFTY

Never Too Busy

"Seek the Kingdom of God above all else, and live righteously,
and he will give you everything you need."

MATTHEW 6:33 NLT

The Bible references Lydia as a successful
businesswoman, a seller of purple cloth. Can you just
imagine the stress of a typical day for her? She ran a
household and a business. She searched for just the right
cloth at just the right price. Then she sought buyers, stern
businessmen and women, who haggled costs and quality.
She bought and transported and delivered cloth. She kept
the books and paid taxes. Whew. This was a woman who
definitely could have used a bubble bath.

That's probably why she knew how important it was to
honor the Sabbath. The Bible says she gathered at the river
to pray with other women, and that's where she heard Paul
share the good news of Jesus. The Lord opened her heart to
Paul's message, and she became a baptized believer. That was
the beginning of her passionate following of Jesus. She was

so supportive of Paul's ministry to tell others about Jesus that she hosted the traveling missionaries in her home.

Making Jesus her number one priority didn't take away her home and business responsibilities, but it must've been such a stress-reliever to give it all to God. Assuming she was baptized in that very river where she'd gathered earlier to pray before she became a believer, can't you just imagine the warmth she felt when she gathered there to pray again?

Lydia was a businesswoman with a lot on her plate, but the Bible says she invited Paul and his companions to her home. She knew that furthering the kingdom of God was more important than other responsibilities.

We can learn a lot from Lydia's priorities. The Bible says that when we put God first in our lives, when we seek his kingdom above all else, God will give us everything we need. We don't need to stress ourselves to succeed. God's idea of success is to seek him. To know him and to make him known. We can change from a stressed worker to a blessed worker when we put God first in our lives. And that's real success.

Dear God, when I have anything other than you at the top of my priorities, my life is a mess. I am stressed and anxious, and I often take out my frustrations on those closest to me. Please help me to keep my priorities in order. God, you deserve my greatest attention and praise. You are worthy to be praised, because you are the one true God and Savior of the world. There is no other like you. Father, no matter how busy I get with family, career, civic obligations, or extracurricular activities, please help me to keep my focus on you. Help me to seek your kingdom above all else. I know that you will take care of the rest.

Do you struggle to keep God first when life gets really busy? When God isn't first in your life, does it create chaos in other areas?

Data from the APA shows that money is the biggest source of stress for Americans, followed by personal relationships, and work.

CHAPTER FIFTY-ONE

Earthquake

I know the LORD is always with me.
I will not be shaken, for he is right beside me.

PSALM 16:8 NLT

Lynn sat on the floor dusting the bookshelf. When the floor began to rumble, she first thought the load of laundry was unbalanced. Before she could stand, she heard her oldest son say, "I'm reading. Stop bouncing the couch." And the two girls, playing in bubbles at the sink, yelled in fear as the chair shook. *Earthquake!*

"Kids, under the table with me, quickly!" Lynn yelled.

The 6.8 magnitude earthquake jolted Seattle, but Lynn and the kids felt the tremors across the Puget Sound in Poulsbo, Washington. She comforted the kids, prayed with them, and then called her mom on the east coast to let her know she was okay.

That night as Lynn soaked in a warm bubble bath trying to ease the stress of the day, she could almost tangibly feel her frayed nerves and residual fears. "God, help," she pleaded.

God reminded her, in a whispered voice to her heart, "Trust me."

Friends, trusting God doesn't mean that bad things won't happen. As the Bible says, there will be trouble in this world: natural disasters, and sometimes bad things caused by humans. One doesn't have to look far to find examples. Earthquakes. Tornadoes. Hurricanes. Lightning strikes. Thunderstorms. Natural disasters can cause a mountain of anxiety and undue fear if we allow it. When we live in a state of worry, dread, or fear, we diminish the power of the Almighty God.

God promises to be with us always, through whatever big or little disaster. He is right beside us, keeping us close, guarding and protecting us. If God allows tragedy from a natural disaster in our lives, he promises to bring good out of that situation. He will never leave us nor forsake us. We can count on that to be true. We can trust his Word, and we can trust him.

God is bigger than any storm, any disaster, any tragedy. God will see us through, and there's a reason his Word says over and over not to be afraid.

Dear God, current events seem to bring me so much angst. From school shootings to floods to kidnappings to tornadoes, it seems like there's so much to worry about, so much to fear. God, you tell me countless times in your Word not to fear. You don't want me to be afraid, for you did not give me a spirit of fear. God, I can trust you to have good plans for me—the best plans—and I don't have to stress no matter what comes my way. You promise to never leave me. You promise to be right by my side. I thank you for those promises because I'll admit that life without you by my side would be the worst tragedy of all.

What fears cause you anxiety? What can serve as a reminder to you that God is always with you?

As with any traumatic event, natural disasters can bring about high levels of stress, anxiety, and anger. Unlike other traumatic events, natural disasters can also result in the tremendous destruction of property and financial loss, further affecting your stress levels and disrupting coping efforts.

CHAPTER FIFTY-TWO

Slaying Giants

David said to the Philistine, "You come against me with sword and spear and javelin, but I come against you in the name of the Lord Almighty, the God of the armies of Israel, whom you have defied. This day the Lord will deliver you into my hands."

1 SAMUEL 17:45–46 NIV

Remember the Bible story of the shepherd boy, David, and the Philistine giant, Goliath? Goliath had been taunting the Israelites for forty days, daring someone to come fight him. To say that the Israelites were stressed was an understatement. Goliath was huge and terrifying, and nobody was brave enough to fight him except that shepherd boy who gathered five smooth stones from the stream.

We all have giants in our lives. Not one named Goliath, but giants of fear and stress. Our finances take a hit or our jobs are threatened and anxiety takes over. We worry about how we'll pay our bills or where we'll find another job.

Health worries also stress us. If you receive one of those

life-altering phone calls from the doctor for you or a loved one, your anxiety levels are off the chart.

The list could go on and on. Stress about how you'll pay for college. Choosing a career path when you get out of school. Finding a sweetheart to spend the rest of your life with. Or even contemplating going through life alone. Maybe your giants include a prodigal child, a fractured relationship with a friend, or a co-worker who keeps causing trouble for you.

Our giants are real and they can rock our world, stressing us to the limit. A mere bubble bath is certainly not enough to calm us down. We need to remember what that shepherd boy did: He wasn't going out to fight Goliath under his own strength, he was going to face the giant armed with God. Everyone else was saying, "Look at the size of the giant." But David was saying, "Look at the size of my God."

That's where our power lies. Giants stress us, but God fights our battles. The next time you're weighed down with stress over situations that you can't fix, go to the one who can. Then go out with his strength and watch as he conquers the situations that stress and worry you.

Lord, I miss the days when I was a little girl and my life could be made instantly better by a bubble bath and a lollipop. I'm tired of fighting giants in my life. I'm tired of giving them power over me. When I'm stressed and I see no way out, remind me that my strength and power is found in you. Remind me of previous times when you've slayed my giants for me. I place my giants—those circumstances that are too big for me—in your hands, knowing that's the best place for them. Give me the courage of David when trials and problems come my way, and instead of focusing on the giants in my life, help me to say, "Look at my God!"

What do you think gave David the courage to stand up to the giant when others wouldn't? Why does it make a difference when you take your eyes off your problems and place them on God?

Giants are not some figment of your imagination. Giants are not something that you dream up. Giants are problems, pressures, pains, and persecutions we have to face from time to time in our lives. Giants often cause major difficulties and bring with them the possibility of life-threatening situations. That's why we need a God who is bigger than every possible giant we face. Trust him today!